It's Go Time

ADVANCE PRAISE

"Jill McAbe's *It's Go Time* translates cutting-edge ideas about how the mind and brain work into everyday language and pragmatic usable strategies. By using concrete examples and exercises, you will get firsthand insight into how to shape your goals and behaviour to start accomplishing more."

—Wil Cunningham, professor of Psychology, University of Toronto

"If you are looking for a nurturing and practical guide to your growth journey in life and business, read Jill McAbe's *It's Go Time.* Jill's well-grounded insights and advice land with authenticity and conviction for they stem from a lifetime of reflection and personal experience."

—Dr. A. R. (Elango) Elangovan, distinguished professor of Organizational Behaviour, Peter B. Gustavson School of Business

"Useful to the extreme. *It's Go Time* is not only a must-read for anyone building an expertise-based business, it's a must-read for anyone who wants to fall in love with their life."

—Giovanni Marsico, CEO/founder of Archangel and executive producer of the Emmy-award winning documentary, *Dreamer*

"A must read for anyone who wants to transition from having a job to owning a business. Jill McAbe's timing is prescient. The Corona Virus pandemic has taught us that we need to seize every opportunity to realize our dreams. With *It's Go Time,* Jill charts a course for how to do exactly that with an insight about how my brain works that opened up doors I didn't know were there."

— Pam Prior, bestselling author of *Your First CFO: The Accounting Cure for Small Business Owners* and CFO to 7- and 8-figure entrepreneurs

"*It's Go Time* is one of the most comprehensive books I have ever read on growing my business. Jill McAbe covers everything from finding your purpose to putting money in your bank account. If you want to wake up excited to run a business that you love every day, buy this book!"

—**Shawna McKinley Robins,** CEO of Kaia Health and Wellness creator of Irresistibly Healthy, and bestselling author of *Powerful Sleep*

"After decades of searching for my purpose, I became resigned to the fact I might not find mine. Then, I read Jill McAbe's *It's Go Time*. Jill combines recent neuroscience, business acumen, and a great deal of wisdom into a system that works. I created my dream business in a matter of months following this system. If you are ready for a better business and life, read this book!"

—**Libby Wildman,** speaker, founder of The Woman's Entrepreneur Collective and creator of Liminal Escapes

"Do you feel like you are meant for more in life? If so, this book might be the key to helping you achieve your full potential. Jill McAbe expertly delivers some of the most actionable insights on how to build an expertise-based business while making your life work the way you want it to. Apply the system you learn from *It's Go Time*, and you'll be unstoppable!"

—**Chris Winfield,** co-founder and CEO at Super Connector Media

IT'S GO TIME

Build the Business and Life
You Really Want

JILL McABE

NEW YORK

LONDON • NASHVILLE • MELBOURNE • VANCOUVER

IT'S GO TIME

Build the Business and Life You Really Want

Published in New York, New York, by Morgan James Publishing. Morgan James is a trademark of Morgan James, LLC. www.MorganJamesPublishing.com

Morgan James BOGO™

A **FREE** ebook edition is available for you or a friend with the purchase of this print book.

CLEARLY SIGN YOUR NAME ABOVE

Instructions to claim your free ebook edition:
1. Visit MorganJamesBOGO.com
2. Sign your name CLEARLY in the space above
3. Complete the form and submit a photo of this entire page
4. You or your friend can download the ebook to your preferred device

ISBN 9781631954344 paperback
ISBN 9781631954351 eBook
Library of Congress Control Number: 2020950782

Cover and Interior Design: Chris Treccani
www.3dogcreative.net

Editor: Cory Hott

Book Coaching: The Author Incubator

Author Photo: Jake Kivanc, jakekivanc.com

Morgan James is a proud partner of Habitat for Humanity Peninsula and Greater Williamsburg. Partners in building since 2006.

Get involved today! Visit
MorganJamesPublishing.com/giving-back

To my CTO and best friend, Samantha.
Thank you for making writing this book the most
natural thing I could have done with my time. (Finally!)

TABLE OF CONTENTS

PREFACE

When I first had the idea to write a book, I expected it would be a straightforward process. I planned to write a book about the science of achieving seemingly impossible goals in which I would share little-known techniques for upgrading your business and life.

When I sat down to write that book, however, I had a case of imposter syndrome. Self-doubt washed over me. Who was I to write such a book? I was standing on the shoulders of giants and thought that it was their work people should be reading.

But the more I met and spoke with scientists and discussed their work, the more I saw their delight in my stories about how their fields of knowledge dovetailed with other disciplines and translated into practice. Some of the researchers I spoke with started calling me a 'science translator,' which helped me realize the distinctiveness of my ability to integrate theory into practice.

As the years went by, I continued to read inspiring research papers and books, yet I never read one that entirely taught me how to achieve what I wanted: To create a service-based business with a great quality of life. So I continued to formulate my success system like a mad scientist might, a dash of this and a sprinkle of that, until I crafted a recipe that was just right for me.

After a few more years of trial and error, thinking, and tinkering, it was time to admit to myself, I had something distinctive to throw into the ring. And, something that worked.

But timing is everything. I released the e-book version of *It's Go Time* on March 12, 2020, the day the record-breaking COVID-19 stock market crash began, now known as Black Thursday. I shook my head at the irony. As we were all being locked down, I released a book titled, *It's Go Time*.

I've trained myself to turn bad news into good. I used the year that followed to continue building my business and the businesses of my clients. It ended up being a record year for many of us. I also used the time to return to the book and contextualize it for a post-COVID-19 economy, which is now more predominantly online than ever before.

After so many years in the making, I would love to hear what you think of *It's Go Time*. If you have an "aha" moment, a question, or a cool story that results from following this system, I hope you will let me know. As you follow this all-in system, my wish for you is that you'll realize new goals, dreams, and potential you didn't know you had in you.

—Jill McAbe
jill@boom-u.com
www.jillmcabe.com
Toronto, Canada

ACKNOWLEDGMENTS

When I was ready to write this book, I expected it to be a solo project. I pictured myself tucked away in a snowed-in chalet, writing day and night for weeks on end until I completed my manuscript. It was nothing like that.

After two years of attempting to write this book on my own, I clued into the truth of the matter: Writing a book that you hope will make a difference, like doing anything of substance, is a team effort. That's when I hired my book coach, Dr. Angela Lauria, to help me clarify my ideas and decide which parts of my story I needed to share. Angela also insisted I use case studies throughout, which leads me to the next set of people I need to thank.

I am deeply grateful to all my students, program participants and clients for choosing me to guide them in transformation. Having hands-on experience was pivotal in my being able to translate science into practical, actionable tools. I would especially like to acknowledge Christine Cowern, Laurie Anne King, Shawna McKinley Robins, and Owen Steinberg for allowing me to share their stories so that readers would have relatable role models.

My father was an economist who instilled a curiosity in me about how the world works. I am thankful for all the academics, scientists, and philosophers who spend their lives deepening our understanding of how our world works. I would particularly like to acknowledge Professors Cunningham and Elangovan for taking the time to share their knowledge and guide the research that led to two of my most pivotal discoveries.

To say I am the author of this book is generous. I am dyslexic, and as such, writing and grammar are not my strongest suits! I am indebted to the diverse editing talents of Joel Baum, Trina Brooks, Bethany Davis, Cortney Donelson, Cory Hott, and Lindsay Stuart, who contributed their unique set of skills to bring clarity to the theories and give life to my stories.

I want to make a special note of thanks to Trina Brooks. Trina is a writer who took my Ignite program. I love hiring former program participants because I know they share my values and understand my unique teachings. We all have Trina to thank for cutting out nonsense, insisting on more examples, and weaving in bits of magic.

I must express my heartfelt appreciation for my partner Professor Joel Baum. Beyond providing the lion's share of editing help with this book, he provided tremendous support to me during my Masters in Leadership and has served as an invaluable advisor during the startup phase of my business, BOOM-U.

I am grateful to Morgan James Publishing for believing in my vision and offering my book a fresh set of wings.

Finally, a note to celebrate my mother, Maria Louise O'Brien: As a special-education trainer, my mother has transformed many lives. No matter how 'unteachable' someone believed they were, she always found a way to help them. Her dedication to helping people achieve things they thought were impossible for them inspired me to build my life on the same principles.

I am where I am today because I have these people and many more like them in my front row. It's impossible to capture in words how grateful I am for the belief, generosity, love, and support of everyone who has been a part of my journey.

CHAPTER 1:

From Uncertain to Unstoppable

W ho comes to mind when you think of a successful entrepreneur? Steve Jobs, who began selling computers out of his parents' garage? Lori Greiner, who patented an earring organizer and went on to create over four hundred consumer products? Perhaps you think of Tesla and SpaceX's leader Elon Musk or *Huffington Post's* founder, Arianna Huffington?

An entrepreneur invents, designs, produces, packages, and sells their products. The more they sell, the greater their success. But what happens when that product is *you*? When what you package and sell is your time, your imagination, your creativity, and your expertise? Where is the entrepreneurial model for building that?

You went into business for yourself because you found something you enjoyed doing and you wanted a certain level of lifestyle freedom. For the longest time, you have worked toward creating your ideal lifestyle and fully believe you would have built it by now. These days, not only have you not achieved the lifestyle goals you set for yourself, you're not sure you're on the right track.

You strive to have a more balanced life, make more consistent money, and solidify your nest egg. The easy part is coming up with ideas. What's been hard is committing enough attention to a course of action. One too many of your past plans didn't pan out as you expected. You have the desire to make a change but are afraid of chasing rainbows again.

Your state of uncertainty is draining. You used to be unstoppable. What you want now is to figure out how to best share your gifts and be confident in your path. Timing-wise, you wanted all this to happen yesterday. Working for yourself was supposed to catapult you ahead, but instead, you feel behind. Is it too late for experimentation? Should you go back to working for someone else? You've thought about it, but even if you found a decent job, there's little chance you'd be paid what you know you're worth.

Besides, you chose to work for yourself because you were committed to living life on your terms. How can you give up now and go to work for someone who doesn't give a fig about you or your future? There's no better option than to get focused, get organized, learn from your mistakes, pick a plan that will pan out, and get busy making it happen.

The Tricky Business of Talent and Time

An income and way of life that fully meet your needs is not a fairy tale, yet to most self-employed experts, coaches, healers, freelancers, and creatives it eventually starts feeling like one.

The number one reason you've been struggling to get your business running like clockwork is that you've been trying to reach the pinnacle of success based on business advice that will only enable you to reach basecamp. And it's not as if getting to basecamp isn't a solid accomplishment. Take Mount Everest, for example. Its basecamp is at 17,600 feet, but the pinnacle—the summit—is at 29,028 feet, a climb that many people attempt and few ever achieve.

The traditional approach to working for yourself got you as far as basecamp, but it's not enough for the next leg of your journey. Most business growth advice does not apply to your situation, which is why so many expertise-based business owners get stuck at a basecamp level of success. You're beyond seeking incremental improvements. You need a way to get to a whole new level—and soon.

What is the pinnacle of success when you sell your talent and time? How about a predictable flow of income doing something you love, enough to meet your financial needs and allow you to live how you choose? If you want to reach this level of success, you're going to need a business-growth system designed expressly for people whose business is selling their expertise. You can think of it as the map you need to climb from basecamp to the summit.

If you have found a vocation you enjoy and would like to lever that into a business you love running, you can join the elite group of expertise-based entrepreneurs at the summit. But to do that, you'll need a system for building your business and becoming incredible with your time—a system designed with people exactly like you in mind.

What Kind of Book Is This?

The main difference between what you will learn in this book and what you will learn in other business and high-performance books—and pay attention, because this is fair warning—is that this system requires you to go deep. There is a master console in your brain where your time and decisions are controlled. If you've tried other popular solutions and they haven't worked, it's because they didn't help you reach your master console. Everything about your success in life and business depends on you getting access to that console.

We are not going to try to fix a power station problem by tinkering with the light switch. We have enough books that give us light-switch solutions. Unfortunately, even the most ingenious of these will disappoint when you have underlying causes that need to be addressed first. When you sell your talent and time, your business and your life are intricately interconnected. You cannot fix one and not the other. We need to treat your business and life as one.

Many people want their work to connect to their life purpose. The desire strengthening with age. The trouble is, if you have a pressing need to make more money to improve your quality of life, you might feel connecting your business to a greater purpose isn't practical. If you have faced this dilemma, I have great news: You don't have to choose. Part of reaching the summit of success requires you to design a business in harmony with your purpose, which is why you'll learn how to discover yours in this book.

When you have confidence in your purpose, you will become clear about what you feel called to create next. It becomes easier to identify which opportunities to act on and which ones to pass on. You'll start building the kind of business that will protect your future while looking after today. You'll enjoy expressing yourself through your work again. You'll smile more.

When you fix problems at the power station rather than the light switch, you fix the problem for good. The system in this book is an all-in system for becoming unstoppable. It is a complete approach to being incredible with your time and transitioning from what you love doing to a business you enjoy running.

Choose Your Adventure

There is a lot in this all-in system (more than my publisher suggested people would want), and that may dissuade some of you from sticking with it. This won't be because it's hard; the steps themselves are easy. What's hard is the inner discovery you'll need to do to take the steps. To make a change in your life, you are going to have to unlearn some of what got you where you are now. Only then will you be free to pursue what you really want.

As you read this book, you will likely encounter ideas that you already know. That may trick you into missing the incredible possibilities awaiting you as you skim for a few new tips. Read more carefully, pay close attention, and apply what you're learning at each step, and you will discover a whole new world and level of success in your business.

We live in a world of hacks, tips, and tricks. There are top ten lists for everything from losing weight to becoming the perfect spouse. We want our business success advice to come just as easily. If we can't digest it in between all our other activities, we won't do it. As the saying goes, "Ain't nobody got time for that."

The quick-fix mindset holds many people back from ever building their dream businesses. The power in the system I'll teach you is not its parts. You can find most of what's in this book in hundreds of places. The power comes from the combination of ideas, how the ideas are linked, and techniques for applying them that most people don't know.

It is said that to know and not do is not to know. This book does not work like a magic wand or Aladdin's lamp. You will not be able to wave it, rub it, or put it under your pillow and expect your ideal business to appear next month. If you read this book looking for tips and tricks, you will surely find them. But if you roll up your sleeves and follow the system, you can expect so much more than that.

With my system, you can expect to build a business that finally fits your lifestyle within two or three years, and if you're diligent, you could build it in perhaps a year or two. However, the most exciting gains from following the system in this book will be that you'll learn how to start enjoying your work—and life—today.

Twenty Years in the Making

After twenty years working for myself and all the ups and downs that entails, I've created a system that makes it possible for people who sell their expertise to achieve levels of motivation, productivity, and success that they never knew they had in them.

The system in this book doesn't come from just one discipline, which is why you haven't seen it before. Parts of the system draw on recent neuroscience and others from behavioral science, change leadership, and management. You'll also find hints of Eastern philosophies, stoicism, and positive psychology, as well as lessons from my twenty-plus years as an entrepreneur, consultant, and coach.

While the individual lessons in this book are standing on the shoulders of giants, this book's power lies in how I've simplified, connected, and sequenced the ideas into a step-by-step system anyone can follow. Over the past two decades, whenever I found an idea, practice, or approach that seemed promising, I tested it in the field, refined it, and integrated it into my work.

Is This Your Go Time?

If you are willing to invest your time as my clients have, then within months of applying the system in this book, you will not recognize yourself or the progress you've made. You can say goodbye to time wasted on projects that lead you down the wrong road. There will be no more second-guessing your decisions about what your next best move should be.

You'll be waking up with energy and excitement. You'll be working on high-value projects you have confidence are the right ones for you. Your productivity will be off the charts. And, before you know it, you're going to need to learn how to invest because you'll need to manage the steady flow of revenue that's coming in. You will be unstoppable.

If all this sounds incredible, you're right. It is. But you will not get there by reading this book at a distance. You need to be all-in.

CHAPTER 2:

A Seemingly-Impossible Goal

At forty-eight, am I too late? That's what I wondered a few years back when I realized—for the third time in a decade—that my work wasn't right for me. I wondered if I'd missed my chance to build my dream business and life. Since a terrible car accident at forty, I'd been obsessed with the idea of finding a way of making money that was perfect for me. I wanted to love what I did and who I did it for, and I wanted lots of time to travel. But there I was, reflecting on yet another idea that didn't pan out and wondering if my dream life was more of a delusion.

If quitting was an option at that point, I might have taken it. The only thought that stressed me more than screwing up another business idea was having an executive job, one where I'd know more and make less than a senior manager fifteen years my junior. If it hadn't been for my car accident, I might have ended up there. But I did have the accident, and ever since, I've fixated on the idea that my life needs to mean something. I wanted to go beyond the limits I had always placed on myself. Taking a corporate job would have meant throwing in the towel on everything I'd believed in and worked toward for eight years.

Entrepreneurship Was in My Blood

I was always destined to work for myself. My parents owned and operated a small private school, and my father's parents had owned a printing shop.

At the age of twenty-nine, I opened my first business with my twin brother: a small bistro in Toronto called JOV. My brother was the chef, and I ran the front of the house. JOV was a sensation right out of the gate. Within months of opening, we achieved international press for our incredible food as well as our leadership in the "trust-the-chef" dining movement. It was a success greater than we could have imagined. Our success fooled me into thinking I knew more about setting up a successful business than I did.

We worked at capacity every day. It pained us to turn away all those reservation requests (often hundreds a day), watching potential revenue go elsewhere. To capitalize on our demand, we came up with the idea of a food shop a few doors up from the bistro. After months of planning, renovating, menu development, and staff training, we opened with high expectations. It was a complete flop. Fast forward another six months, and we had tinkered with the food shop enough to eke out a small profit, but there was no joy in it. We closed the shop.

My Leadership Lab

With our focus back on the restaurant, we had a conundrum. Our business was too small for us, but we were leery of going after something else. I needed something to occupy myself. That's when I began studying leadership and business in more depth. To avoid repeating my past mistakes, I took courses, read books, and, more importantly, used my restaurant as a "lab" to apply what I was learning.

The more I learned and experimented with operational fine-tuning, the more fascinated I became and the more I yearned to try out my skills and ideas on other projects. After seven successful years running our business, my brother and I agreed the bistro was not enough for us anymore. We still lacked the confidence to add a second business, so we sold the restaurant to explore new opportunities.

An Involuntary Life Reset

After taking some well-deserved time off to travel, I returned to Toronto and hung out my shingle as a hospitality consultant, but that plan was thwarted almost as quickly as it began. Within the year, my life was turned upside down.

In April 2009, a driver on his cell phone ran a red light and T-boned my car. During 2009 and 2010, I learned firsthand how life could be redirected in an instant. I suffered agonizing pain from my spine, neck, and brain injuries caused by the accident. Activities I used to enjoy became unbearable. Everything hurt—sitting, standing, and sleeping. I couldn't cook or go to the gym. I stopped seeing friends and family. I became a recluse.

As I emerged from that year and a half of pain, loneliness, and depression, I vowed to make the most of my life from then on. I was done with "good enough." Before the accident, I had ticked all the boxes—a swanky condo with a waterfront view, a hip boyfriend, and exotic vacations—but now it all seemed so surface level. They brought me little sense of meaning. I wanted something more. I wanted to make a difference.

I was at a crossroads, and I knew it. I was in the wrong career, the wrong relationship, the wrong life. Although I was ready for a new one, I still felt trapped by the life I was in. The accident caused me to lose everything I had built and put me in considerable medical debt. Despite sensing hospitality consulting was not for me, I got a high-profile contract, and it paid my bills for two years.

The company was terrific, and I adored the owner and the team. It had all the potential for me to go full-time, but something in me just wouldn't let me do it. I had a gnawing feeling that I was living the wrong life. A voice in my head kept whispering, "This is not as it should be." I couldn't put my finger on what was off, but I trusted the whispers.

I Couldn't Settle for Less

I knew I had to get out of the restaurant industry. I knew I had a purpose and calling that were just for me and that I wasn't on the right path yet. Being a sidekick in someone else's dream wasn't going to work for me. After nearly losing it all, I knew I wanted it all. But I was forty-five years old, a dyslexic who barely graduated high school, a university drop-out, and highly credible in an industry I wanted to leave.

I was going to need new credentials while still working to pay the bills, and I needed a better way to manage my time. Like most people looking for change, I turned to business and self-help books. I read about time management, resilience, goal setting, and so much more. I read the classics and countless new authors, too. Many boiled down to similar advice: Clarify what you want and then work hard to make it happen. Although I did make progress, I couldn't figure out my purpose and calling, so how could I truly clarify what I wanted?

Determined, I pressed on, turning my attention to more academically-minded books and programs. Professionally, I obtained certifications in executive coaching, team coaching, personal assessments, communication, and change leadership. I eventually went back to university and earned my Master of Arts in Leadership.

My plan worked. I broke free of hospitality consulting and started getting engagements with entrepreneurs in a broad range of industries. Applying my training, I had jaw-dropping successes. Burnt-out teams would come to life, taking on projects and succeeding where they'd previously stalled. People who thought they couldn't work together would. Productivity levels thought impossible weren't.

In many ways, it was work I loved, but it wasn't a lifestyle I loved. Long hours, rush hour treks to and from distant industrial parks, always worrying about how and when I'd find my next client. Worst of all, I was helping clients add millions to their top lines, and I was selling my time by the hour. I was supposed to be gaining control over my life; instead, I'd built myself a business with no leverage and a lifestyle that controlled me. I gave my head a shake.

It had been eight years since my accident and my commitment to a dream life, and I still hadn't come close to figuring out my perfect business or life. Here I was, an expert in helping established entrepreneurs grow their businesses to their next level of success with less personal effort … while being unable to do it for myself.

The irony was sickening. My spirits were flattened. I was forty-eight, my career had started with such promise, and I felt like an utter failure, wondering if I would ever catch up.

A Last Ditch Attempt

At my wit's end, I decided to become my own growth consultant. The challenge I faced was that my training was for organizations, not individuals selling their talent and time. I couldn't find a business model for someone like me. Business education tended to teach how to build product, tech, or large consulting businesses, and self-help didn't cover business matters adequately. I tried several coaching programs, but none solved the problems that troubled me most: What was I meant to do and how could I have a great income *and* quality of life doing it?

It became clear that what I wanted wasn't out there in a book or online program, so it was going to be up to me. I needed to meld the business and personal growth advice I gained over the years into a single, all-in system for people who sold their talent and time. When you are the business and the business is you, you cannot flourish unless both sides are involved.

I decided to pull everything I'd learned into a complete system, adapt it to my needs, and connect the ideas in a logical sequence, each step building on the next. I knew from my consulting experience that correct sequencing was where the power would come from.

My approach was also going to have to be detailed. In my experience, self-directed learning was heavy on what I should do and light on how to do it. That just doesn't work for my dyslexic brain. When I started adapting my organizational tools for myself, I took comfort in detailing clear instructions and best practices for how to do things.

As I became my own client, I still harbored fears that I was going to blow it again. But I forced myself to keep the faith. After all, I had guided remarkable transformations for complex business organizations. Surely I could get some of those benefits for myself?

I started at square one, unwilling to skip a step no matter how difficult or uncomfortable. After years of trying, a new approach led to me figuring out my purpose. Once I understood my purpose, I realized the impact I wanted to make and the business I wanted to build. From there, I used my change leadership knowledge to create a personal achievement tool so that as I moved forward with any goal—no matter how unfamiliar the task or situation—I could navigate to a successful outcome.

Third Time's the Charm

The first success story of the system I developed was me. After clarifying my purpose and vision, I launched BOOM-U, an online business school with a mission to help solo-entrepreneurs grow themselves, their income, and their impact.

BOOM-U is a different kind of online school. Instead of mass-market education where everything is recorded, we offer courses and programs that include personalized attention, feedback from highly trained coaches, and program design that leads to exceptionally high success rates. At the time of writing, our two signature programs are Ignite: Activate Your Big Idea and Basecamp: Increase Your Impact with a Signature Program.

Ignite is for people who have an idea about working for themselves but are feeling stuck because they aren't entirely clear on the idea or how they could implement it. Basecamp is for solo-entrepreneurs who have years of experience in their field and want to create a proprietary teaching or coaching system based on their work. We also offer programs that help graduates of Ignite and Basecamp set up their sales and marketing systems, financial management systems, and learn how to grow their teams when the time comes.

After all those years, I finally created a business that is perfect for me. With BOOM-U, I get to do what I love, collaborate with experts and industry leaders who energize me, and create a community for people who are making the world a better place! My team and I pour our hearts into serving our clients and program participants, but our evenings and weekends are our own. I enjoy long walks on the beach with my dogs, I travel often and run my business from anywhere.

The changes in my life have been nothing short of revolutionary. I earn more, enjoy my work more, and wake up (almost) every day feeling invigorated by the day ahead. I still have dreams I've yet to realize, but I no longer feel like I'm in the wrong life. I know I'm finally on my right path.

Harder Than Necessary

Getting to this point was much harder than it needed to be. It shouldn't have taken me the better part of a decade to create a business and life that I enjoyed. Looking around, I realized that just about everyone I knew with a service-based business was in the same boat I used to be in—pretending (and hoping) things were going better than they were.

Since I now knew it was possible to have a happy and healthy life when your business involves selling your talent and time, I needed to make sure what worked for me would work for others. Offering my coaching services to other service-based entrepreneurs, I taught them the early version of the system I will teach you in this book.

The Right Time

After iterating my process several times, my system started yielding predictable results. Regardless of their industries, burnt-out business owners unsure of what to do next who followed the system would become clear, confident, and reinvigorated as they finally understood a clear path to getting to their desired results.

That's when I knew I had to get the word out with a book. I wanted everyone with a service-based business to understand how to go from overwhelmed and uncertain to making a great living doing what they love.

When you follow this system, you can do more than build a reliable business. Because of what I teach you about your brain and the science of achievement, bigger goals in all aspects of your life become possible. You will achieve levels of motivation, creativity, and productivity that will change how you live, work, socialize and succeed. This system goes beyond your business; it's an all-in system for unlocking your potential.

No matter where you are on your journey, no matter if things got bleak for you as they did for me, and no matter if you're wondering, as I did, whether it's too late for you to catch up—it's not. If you are committed to doing work you love while also enjoying your life, you can achieve this. One consultant who attended a live seminar of mine booked a million-dollar contract the week after learning a fraction of what I will teach you here. An intuitive counselor who took Basecamp tripled her sales in her first quarter after graduating.

What you will learn in this book is not about a quick fix. It's an all-in system for people who *are* the product, selling their time, imagination, creativity, and expertise. It's for experts, coaches, healers, creatives, and anyone rethinking their life, exploring their options, and struggling with the question, "How do I make my business work?"

If that's you, this book will help you clarify your direction, reignite your motivation, unpack what you are meant to do, and teach you how to transition from what you love doing to the owner of a business you love running.

Ready to learn what I mean when I say this system is all-in?

CHAPTER 3:

The All-In System

When Christine, a successful Toronto real estate agent, came to me several years ago, she needed to rethink how she operated. Christine's sales results were impressive but achieving them took a toll on her quality of life. She wanted to transition from being a typical time-strapped real estate agent to running a business that afforded her a desirable quality of life, but she couldn't see what her options were or what she should do next.

Being a real estate agent is inherently inefficient. Much of the work takes place in the evenings and on weekends, in addition to traveling to locations all over the city, meeting deadlines, and, in Toronto, high-pressure time-sensitive bidding wars.

When I first met Christine, she regularly worked all hours of the day and was constantly exhausted. She knew this had to change but couldn't see how to do it. Christine enjoyed real estate, but she was unwilling to give up on her dream of a better quality of life. She was determined to build a business that she loved running. Like most expertise entrepreneurs, she was limited by the idea that there was a fixed set of rules by which real estate agents had to conduct their business and that her clients wouldn't have it any other way.

I asked Christine to set aside, for the moment, all of the constraints she felt the outside world imposed on how things are or should be and invited her to focus solely on what she wanted for her future. Released from these constraints, Christine was able to get clear about the kind of business she wanted to own down the road. She realized she wanted to level up the real estate business by delivering a white-glove service that would blow her clients away. To do that, she needed to reorganize workflow so her team members would also have lives they loved.

Once Christine understood what she wanted for her future, clients, and team, there was no option but to build it. What initially seemed to Christine to be unbreakable rules were, in fact, opportunities to catapult her team into a league of their own. Using the performance equation I'll teach you in this book, Christine systemized her business and claimed back time that was formerly wasted. She then reinvested that time in her three top priorities: providing white-glove service for her clients, developing a high-performing, self-managing team, and systemizing marketing.

In a few short years, the Christine Cowern Real Estate Team has disrupted the real estate business in ways I have not heard of before. For example, they created a concierge service that helps clients with any home-related goal or challenge for as long as they own their homes. Her team has grown to seven people, along with several contractors. Her referral rate, which was already impressive, doubled, and she is consistently ranked in the top 2 percent of real estate agents in Toronto—no small feat with over 52,000 agents in the city.

But to my clients and me, success is never about just numbers. It's also about our quality of life. Christine now has that, too. No more working late into the night and on weekends. That time belongs to her husband and their new baby. The Christine Cowern Real Estate Team runs like clockwork with one of her first hires, now her managing partner, at the helm. When I called to fact-check the details for this story, Christine was happily packing for a week-long getaway at a Pilates retreat in Nicaragua.

If Christine had followed the original path she was on, she would have burnt out in a matter of years. Instead, in just over three years, Christine created value for her clientele leagues beyond what anyone would expect from their real estate agent, a high-performing, self-managing team, and a healthy work-life balance for herself.

You can do this, too. Like Christine when she started with me, all you need to get going is the commitment to make it happen and a path to follow that makes your goal possible.

Four Options for How to Make a Living

Robert T. Kiyosaki, the best-selling author of *Rich Dad, Poor Dad*, is well known for a model he calls the "cash flow quadrant" that he uses to illustrate the four ways you can choose to make money:

1. An employee: working for, and at the mercy of, someone else or a corporation
2. Self-employed: you own a job, and your income disappears if you need to step away
3. A business owner: the owner of a system that can make money with or without you
4. An investor: you get money working for you instead of working for money

In Kiyosaki's view, being an employee is undesirable because your income depends on the mercy of others. He is even less favorably disposed toward being self-employed because when you work alone, your income disappears if you need to step away from the business. Kiyosaki encourages people toward the last two options: Become a business owner, at minimum, and ideally, become an investor.

Before my car accident, I did not understand the urgency of Kiyosaki's advice the way I do now. I learned the hard way that we are not always in control of when we will and won't be able to work. Most of my clients have had situations that have caused them to step back from work, too. Yet if you ask most self-employed people if they'd rather be a business owner or continue their current situation, they will likely tell you that building a business is beyond the level of hassle they want.

That's how I felt back at forty-eight. Back then, I only knew about traditional business growth models. In my case, as a change consultant, that would have meant building a B2B (business to business) training and consulting company that would be a headache to manage. A complicated business was not my idea of an ideal life. Back then, I couldn't imagine a business that would be less work and more fun than selling my time by the hour.

If you have felt the same, I have good news for you. The Internet has introduced possibilities that can increase the value you provide while minimizing the effort you need to expend, and many larger businesses have been slow to adapt! This gap creates opportunities for people like you and me. Integrating the Internet's power into your service delivery will require ingenuity, but with a system that shows you the way, you can figure it out.

The All-In System for Becoming Unstoppable

Indeed, there are several steps to follow to transition from being self-employed to becoming the owner of a business that you feel is perfect for you. But it doesn't need to be daunting. Work is daunting when you're not sure what project to choose or how to speed up success. When you have confidence in what projects you're choosing, and you know how to do more in less time, work can be fun. That's why I created the all-in system I teach you in this book.

Confidence Choosing Projects

When your time is your product, building a business that will be perfect for you starts with clarifying what matters to you most and how you define a life well-lived. Discovering your purpose, envisioning what you want for your future, and committing to the kind of person you want to become are three critical puzzles you need to solve. When you don't know these things about yourself, it becomes hard—if not impossible—to build a business that will sustain *you*.

Once you're centered on who you are and the kind of life you want to live, you will be surprised at how much easier it is for you to clarify—and have confidence in—the sort of business you want. With your business vision clarified, you can turn your attention to filling in the gap between where you are now and where you want to be with a series of well-chosen projects.

Using a tool I call the Expertise Business Growth Model (EBGM), you will get new clarity and insight about how to choose the most opportune projects at each stage of your business development. How long it takes you to reach your ultimate destination, your business vision, will depend on how well you execute each project. For example, someone with a Ferrari and someone with a Fiat could share a destination and know the shortest route, but the person with the better tool—in this case, the Ferrari—will arrive sooner.

Do More in Less Time

When it comes to project execution, most people have learned Fiat-level tools. Fiat-level performance tools are sufficient for projects you already know how to crush. The problem is they don't set you up for success when you have to tackle projects in areas where you have little or no experience. Following the EBGM, you can expect to excel at projects in disciplines that are new (or unfamiliar) to you.

There are Ferrari-level approaches to achievement; these are the approaches you need to use when you want your success to be inevitable, or when speed matters. The second part of the all-in system in this book will teach you a Ferrari-level performance equation that makes you a master of crushing projects in record time.

When you are clear on who you want to become and where you want to end up, you will be able to design a business that's right for you. Once you have clarified your business vision, the EBGM will be your guide to choosing the right projects at the right time. And, using a Ferrari-caliber performance equation, you'll crush your projects in record time. You'll be running your ideal business before you know it. This is the all-in system for success.

All-In: Choose Better Projects with the EBGM

Is it possible to have too much of a good thing? It can be when those things are ideas or projects to tackle on the road to success. The dilemma is which project is the logical next best step when all of them show promise. As you are reading this, you are probably agonizing over a dozen different projects. Wouldn't it be nice if you could just wiggle your nose and have your brand strategy, graphic design, systemization, content marketing, social media, funnels, advertising, administration, and public relations all fall into place?

You can indeed build a terrific business one project at a time, but there's an order of operations that will multiply your success. Attempt projects in the wrong order, and you often find yourself set back.

While elements of what you will learn in this book are taught in business schools, few service-based entrepreneurs realize how the path to building a business applies to them too. To fill this gap, I developed the Expertise Business Growth Model (EBGM), an approach people who sell their talent and time can follow to transition from owning a job to owning a business.

I've always likened achieving challenging goals to climbing mountains, which is why I chose the basecamp analogy at the opening of the book. The first climb in the EBGM is from ground zero to basecamp; the second climb is from basecamp to the summit.

EBGM: From Ground Zero to Basecamp, Owning a Job

Ground zero is where everyone starts. As we grow up, adults ask us what we want to do for a living. Most of us try several things until we find something that we enjoy enough to settle on. With this decision made, we turn our attention to training. We take programs and courses, earn degrees or certifications, and seek to apprentice with the best.

Eventually, we decide to work for ourselves and start taking clients. The first ones tend to come as lucky breaks; then, we build on that. Reaching this level of success is what I call reaching basecamp: you have developed skill-sets and made money sharing your expertise. But, business isn't consistent, so you've started to develop your business know-how by reading blogs and books or taking courses and coaching programs in the hopes it will help you stabilize your results.

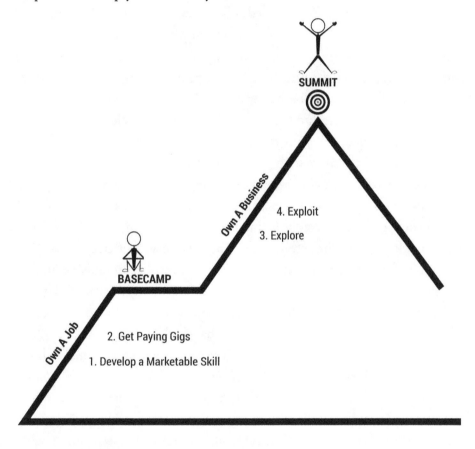

The Risk of Camping Out at Basecamp

For the first little while, basecamp feels terrific. You worked hard to get this far, you own your job, you found something you love to do, and you feel like you're in charge of your world. But the longer you remain at basecamp, the more frustrated, time-strapped, and burnt-out you tend to become. One reason for this is that the more skilled you are in your field, the more you will want to raise your rates to match your competence. Indeed, you probably misquoted some of your earlier jobs and ended up working so many evenings and weekends to get the job done that you are working for less than you'd make working at Starbucks.

The trouble is that as you raise your rates, you often move out of competition with other job owners and into competition with business owners. It's hard for self-employed job owners to compete with business owners. Business owners often create offerings and efficiencies, like Christine Cowern's concierge service, that are impossible for someone working on their own to match. But, if you don't raise your rates, you may start wondering if you would be better off working at Starbucks and at least getting free coffee, tea, and benefits. Keeping your rates low may also lead your clients to question your competence—why, despite your experience, are your fees competitive with people just starting out?

Another risk of staying at basecamp too long is that, whether or not you raise your rates, clients get harder and harder to find. Self-employed job owners often mistakenly blame this on changes in the market. They start making course corrections, tweaking their service offerings, changing the type of clients they serve, or both. In truth, this is more like climbing back down to ground zero. Each time you pivot what you offer and, more critically, for whom you offer it, you confuse your market and make it difficult for your community to know what you're up to.

As Ogilvy advertising legend Rory Sutherland explains in his book *Alchemy: The Dark Art and Curious Science of Creating Magic in Brands, Business, and Life,* you don't need to be the best to win more business; you just need to be less risky than your clients' other options. When you change your business idea or niche, your community doesn't know what to think of you. It makes it risky for your past clients to recommend you and harder for would-be clients to discover you. Each time you pivot, you help your competition become the less risky choice.

How Do You Move Beyond Basecamp?

It's time to plan your exit from basecamp when you've found something you love doing but your working situation and lifestyle are not what you want them to be. When Christine came to me, she loved real estate but not the hours or stress. By reinventing the norms in her industry, she built a business that affords her a great quality of life. If you have a skill you feel is right for you and a work life that is wrong for you, then it's time to move to the exploration step of the EBGM—figuring out a business idea and niche you can commit to for at least three years.

EBGM: From Basecamp to the Summit, Owning a Business

Before ascending from basecamp to the summit, you need to prepare for the journey. Some people may grab their pack and set off running, confident in their skills and direction. Others prefer to explore the different routes and tools at their disposal, wary of finding themselves halfway up a mountain only to realize the path they chose was a dead end. One way to think about how to go about building a business you'll enjoy running is through the lens of the exploration and exploitation phases of building a business.

In the exploration phase, you create a proprietary or signature solution and test its marketability to ensure its viability for the climb to the summit. Your service (aka product) development, verifying market appetite, and getting sales are among the activities that focus on this phase. Critically, the exploration phase is where you commit to a target market. Viability means you have a proven way of reaching your market, making sales, and being profitable.

Once you have proven the viability of an idea, you can advance to the exploitation phase. Exploitation activities have to do with efficiency and expansion. Since you have locked down your main business idea and niche, you can now focus on creating standard operating procedures (SOPs) to simplify all aspects of your business operations. It makes sense that you will be able to develop standards once what you sell is standardized. Standardizing your processes is a key to becoming the owner of a system that can make money with or without you.

The exploitation phase is also where you pick up a megaphone and tell everyone what you do through activities such as marketing, advertising, and public relations. Until you've locked in on what you will sell and to whom, intensive marketing, advertising, and public relations can confuse your market and make it harder for you to gain credibility in your chosen market when you are ready. You're better off going through the exploration phase five or ten times than jumping into the exploitation phase too early. Once you have established an idea is viable, you can move to exploit it quickly.

Timing Is Everything

When it comes to being immeasurably better with your time, one of the smartest things you can do is pick the right project for the right time. When you do the right work at the wrong time, you will not get the benefit you anticipated. You will end up spending time and money on things you didn't need and, eventually, find yourself needing to redo the work when the time is right.

When you know what projects you should take on and at what time, goals that might have seemed initially far-fetched go from appearing out of reach to well within your grasp. Once you know what projects to pick, a performance equation will help you speed up success.

Christine achieved success because she understood that to go from working independently to becoming the owner of a business she could step away from, she needed to develop new competencies and tackle different kinds of projects. The performance equation I share in this book helped her to speed up her learning curve.

All-In: Achieve More with a Performance Equation

Have you ever heard the expressions "change is hard" or "you can't teach an old dog new tricks?" If you have, it wasn't from someone in the field of behavioral science or change leadership. The idea that change is next to impossible is about as accurate as saying "making a soufflé is impossible" or "only professional chefs can make soufflés." While this fluffy baked egg dish is a level of culinary expertise relatively few people are skilled in, it doesn't mean it's an unattainable goal.

Many endeavors are hard or unlikely without the proper technique, recipe, or equation. When it comes to change, there is an equation—a series of steps you can follow—that will make change inevitable in even the most challenging circumstances. No component of this equation is particularly difficult. What's challenging is that few people outside the profession of behavioral science or change leadership are aware of all the steps involved.

During my years working in entrepreneurial organizations, I became used to resistance from directors and VPs from the very start. I didn't let this bother me because I knew that after a few days of working together, they would be asking to work with me again. How did I come to expect this shift in their disposition? Who doesn't love someone who makes it *easier* for them to achieve *more*? In my experience, when you show someone clear steps they can follow to perform at their best, they are happier, and happier people produce more. It's a positive reinforcement cycle.

Although I could predict that it would be a matter of days before management teams looked forward to their time with me, I reflected on how I might reframe our introductions to be more harmonious from the start. I understood that, to somebody untrained, the idea of change seems daunting. I considered whether the word "change" inherently suggested that something was wrong and needed to be corrected.

A New Perspective on Change

We tend to associate the need for change with the idea that things are broken and need to be fixed. As a result, it's not surprising that management teams don't jump up and down shouting, "Yippee!" when a change leadership consultant struts in promising productivity utopia in the months ahead. If I were in their shoes, I suspect I'd be apprehensive, too.

I began thinking about how we needed to shift the concept of change to one of improvement. Why couldn't we take a growth-oriented point of view instead? If we did, we'd celebrate where we were and how far we had come, treating every moment as an opportunity to progress from where we are into what we have the potential to become.

With this reframing, I realized my training in change was just an education in how to make seemingly impossible goals happen. It was a scientific approach that had little to do with how most people and teams approach their goals. I redeveloped my change equation into a high-performance tool I call MINDCODE®. The new framing paid off. As I had hoped, leaders and teams were more receptive to the idea that I could help provide better structure to their planning and implementation efforts.

I include MINDCODE® as part of Ignite and Basecamp and used to use it when working with larger organizations. Project managers and high performers adore it because it simplifies and systemizes the critical steps to getting more done on shorter timelines while also demystifying how to approach complex projects. At BOOM-U, we use it to plan and execute all our projects. The performance equation I teach you in this book is based on MINDCODE®.

Your All-In Project-Crushing System

To build a successful business, you need to become adept at navigating unknown territory. Like a journey up Mount Everest, every new elevation requires a level of knowledge beyond the level you needed to get to where you are now. As you move up the EBGM toward building a business you love running, so will other competitors in your space. To gain or maintain competitive advantage, you will need to continually develop your knowledge and abilities to keep pace.

A step-by-step performance equation ensures you accomplish whatever you set your mind to in the shortest possible amount of time.

The power of the performance equation in this book results from two key differences in how most people approach achieving goals. The first is the sequencing of the steps—the equation. The second is the technique.

Just as a soufflé will miss the mark without the cream of tartar, ignoring any step in a performance equation can lead to disappointing results, even when you get all the other steps right.

The Problem of Missing Pieces

When I break down past project failures with my clients, we often find they were doing an excellent job at the things they knew to do, and what held them back was that they were missing necessary pieces of the puzzle. The second difference in the performance equation in this book is the focus on technique. One thing that frustrates my dyslexic brain is being told *what* I should do, complete with convincing arguments as to *why* I should do it, with relatively little guidance on *how* I should do it.

Anders Ericsson, one of the foremost researchers on learning faster and the lead author of *Peak: How to Master Anything*, instructs us that those who outperform others in their fields focus on a type of practice he's termed "deliberate practice," which stipulates the need for expert technique.

In all disciplines, there are degrees of excellence. Some people are better than others at playing piano, chess, soccer, tennis, riding bicycles, making omelets, designing buildings, knitting, singing, or sewing. What separates these top performers? Ericsson stresses the importance of starting with proven techniques under the direction of an expert teacher or coach. His ideas have been instrumental in my commitment to developing best-in-class techniques for achieving goals.

The Four Phases of Crushing Projects

Whenever someone tells me how hard they are working on a goal, I know they are not using a science-based performance equation. Hard work does not suggest optimal performance. It indicates a person is expending more energy than required only to achieve results below their potential. When you apply the performance equation in this book to any project you are working on, you will be amazed at how much more you accomplish and how much more natural success feels.

The four phases of the performance equation are:

- Phase I: Coordinates of Your Current Location (Chapters 4 and 5)
- Phase II: Clarification of Your Target Destination (Chapters 6 and 7)
- Phase III: Plans for an Easier Approach (Chapters 8 and 9)
- Phase IV: Practices to Speed up Ascension (Chapters 10 and 11)

Phase I: Coordinates of Your Current Location

Like many people, I used to believe the first step of success was setting a goal. How wrong I was! During my master's program, I realized that the first step of achievement is understanding where you are now and how you arrived at this destination. During the first two weeks of the program, my classmates and I were guided through a series of activities to help us learn these things about ourselves. It was deep, soul-searching work that led many of us to revelations about ourselves we were not anticipating in a leadership program.

No one escaped those two weeks without shedding tears, not even our tougher classmates in the military and police services. We were required to complete these activities because, as we learned, you cannot hope to lead or bring about the best in others if you cannot first lead or bring about the best in yourself. When it comes to leading yourself or others, it makes sense that it is harder to get anywhere new if you don't start by determining your starting position. In Chapters 4 and 5, you will discover your current coordinates from two vantage points.

First, we'll look back to reveal how you've come to get to where you are today, which we'll examine through the lens of neuroscience. In Chapter 4, "Your Brain and Your Current Reality," you'll discover why you've felt blocked in some areas of your life, why you see, say, and do what you do. You'll learn why some goals have eluded you, and you'll be introduced to a part of your brain that you can program to help you automatically work toward any goal of your choosing.

Second, we'll explore what brings you happiness and reveal how you can create a greater sense of meaning and joy in your future. In Chapter 5, "Your Happiness Recipe," you'll discover your purpose and your vision for your life and business. We'll also take a look at value-driven behaviors you can introduce to speed up getting from where you are now to where you want to be.

Phase II: Clarification of Your Target Destination

With an understanding of where you are now and where you'd like to be down the road, it will be time to pick a project that will get you on the shortest route to your destination. In Chapters 6 and 7, I teach you the power-practice of exploring possibilities before you commit, followed by brain-based techniques for goal setting that have the power to make you unstoppable.

There are slower and faster routes to getting anywhere. Like a climber tackling Mount Everest, at each decision point, you have an opportunity to choose a more or less challenging path. I call the project you will identify in Phase II a "leap project" because when you identify the right one, like when you discover a shorter path, you will be amazed how quickly you advance. In Chapter 6, "Where to Next?" we'll take a closer look at the EBGM and consider some common scenarios that will empower you to make a wise choice about what your leap project should be.

Most people with even a modicum of ambition know that goal setting is job number one once you've identified a project you want to achieve. In my decade of experience helping entrepreneurs build their businesses and teaching thousands of students online, I can confidently say that it is a rare individual who knows how to set a goal so it has power. In Chapter 7, "Who Needs Willpower?" I teach you how to create goals with power. You'll learn about recent advances in neuroscience and how to set "hot goals" in your subconscious. Why do you need to set goals in your subconscious? Because when your subconscious isn't aware of your goals, you'll either work far harder than necessary or won't achieve your goals at all. When you've set a hot goal in your subconscious, you'll know it because you'll be working toward your goal without willpower.

Phase III: Plans for an Easier Approach

As Dwight D. Eisenhower famously said, "In preparing for battle, plans are useless, but planning is indispensable." This is the attitude we will take toward planning in Chapters 8 and 9. Properly done, the value of planning is not about creating a plan itself, but rather the mental preparation that grooms your brain to gain exacting clarity about what you want and see your projects through to completion on shorter timelines.

Our approach will be based in behavioral science. In Chapter 8, "Better Road Maps," you'll learn the minimum effective dose for creating better plans. First, you'll create a back-of-the-napkin "staircase" strategy: a road map of subprojects that gives your subconscious (and you) confidence that your leap project is not only plausible but also inevitable. Then you'll drill down into a component of your leap project we call your "active assignment" as we create the nitty-gritty detail portion of your plan.

Based on your past experiences, your subconscious can throw up roadblocks when it deems a project overly ambitious. In Chapter 9, "Prepare for Challenging Terrain," you will learn planning techniques necessary to approach projects where you have little or no prior experience or where you have subconscious blocks to success. You will develop contingency plans and take a microscope to your limiting social environments and beliefs as you learn how to circumvent the elements of your thought patterns and life that are currently limiting you from achieving more.

Your world is perfectly organized for the results you're currently getting. When you've completed Phase III, you'll understand the science of rearranging your world to get any results you want from now on.

Phase IV: Practices to Speed up Ascension

I am frequently asked for training on time management. You will learn how to be more productive in Chapters 10 and 11 of this book; however, I don't call what you will learn here "time management." Here's why: When you start with the wrong question, you get the wrong answer. Google dictionary defines "management" as "the process of dealing with or controlling things or people." We cannot control time. Go ahead. Try to turn back time five minutes. I'll wait.

Time is a resource you can liken to money. It's something you can invest wisely or not so wisely. To me, investing your time wisely means you can look back on how you spent your week, month, year, or life and say to yourself, "I feel great about my life and how I lived." Seriously, what is the point of spending a minute on anything you'll end up regretting?

In Chapters 10 and 11, you're going to learn to love your time now. This hour, today. Not next week or month. Not someday. When you approach your time with the practices I will teach you in Phase IV, execution starts to feel more natural. It's not that you won't have to work to make your goals happen; it's that it will feel easier to do the work—even enjoyable.

In Chapter 10, "The Dopamine Drip," you'll learn how to reward and motivate yourself with dopamine. Dopamine is a neurotransmitter your body produces each time you take action on your top priority goals. This release of dopamine initiates a positive reinforcement cycle, triggering your subconscious to take more actions that produce dopamine. I'll teach you daily and weekly time practices that release dopamine as you work toward your goals. If you practice what you learn in this chapter, working on things you care about will soon feel like the most natural thing you could be doing with your time.

No performance equation would be all-in without tools and techniques to turn things around when your efforts don't work out as planned. When it comes to things not working out—or failure, as some people prefer to label it—there is a disconnect between the high-performance wisdom to embrace failure and how the real world responds to it. In Chapter 11, "The Elephant in the Room," you will learn recovery tools that you can think of as your emergency kit to keep you on track to success. These tools include protocols for overcoming fear, resistance, and significant setbacks. Not only will the protocols you learn in this chapter teach you the steps to turn disappointing situations to your advantage, but they'll also show you how to convert your setbacks into stories of conquest that become the very reasons for your success.

How to Become Unstoppable

I'm not going to mislead you—some experts suggested I write two books because getting through this material will take dedication and patience that, according to some, most people don't have. But I decided to write one book. I can't solve your problems with two books unless you read both of them, and that seemed inefficient to me. Our Basecamp participants handle the material without issue. Far from being overwhelmed, they are relieved when they finally gain clarity on how to build the business they've wanted for years. So I know that if you have the problems that I share how to solve in this book, you'd probably rather not go on a wild goose chase, reading two or more books when I had the option to include what you need in one.

We live in a world of targeted, fragmented information and quick tips. I am a fan of targeted expertise, quick fixes, tips, and tricks myself. But tips and tricks only help when you know the basic structure of how to do something. If you wanted to become a mountain climber, would you learn by patching together tips from here and there? I hope not—without proper training, you could meet an untimely end. Once you had learned the mountain climbing foundations, would targeted tips and tricks be of value? Absolutely.

It takes commitment and follow-through to succeed at building an expertise-based business from the ground up, but I know that if you invest your time in applying this all-in system, you will notice the benefits right away. Follow the system in this book, and within one to two years you can transition from owning a job to owning a business that makes the lifestyle you dream of your reality.

The Best Way to Read this Book

I suggest you start by reading the book through from cover to cover to understand the system in its entirety. Then I suggest using this as a handbook starting with Chapter 4, following the steps and activities in each chapter as needed to guide your business development.

Resist the urge to put the book down and jump into action when you get excited about new ideas bubbling to the surface. I've seen people quit partway through and then end up struggling without knowing why or how to correct their course. A proven way to increase your chances of success is to find a success buddy—a friend you think is also ready to build a better business—so you can support each other as you do your climb.

The Rabbit Hole

One of the hardest tasks in the restaurant business is not deciding what goes on a menu; it's deciding what to leave off. I used that same approach here. Everything you will learn in this book works because the system stands on the shoulders of giants. Throughout the book, I refer to the work of some of my most meaningful influences. But this book is not about theories or research. It is about a practical system for action based on their work.

To cover the wide range of topics behind the system, I had to leave a lot out, but I know your curious mind will want to understand at least some of the book's ideas at a deeper level. I've done my best to give you enough background to apply the material successfully at each step of the system. But in case you find your inquiring mind calling out to you, I've created an online resource I call The Rabbit Hole.

The name "The Rabbit Hole" is inspired by *Alice in Wonderland*, and you can find it at https://www.jillmcabe.com/itsgotime_rabbit. If you want to go deeper into a given topic or chapter, The Rabbit Hole is where you'll find some of my favorite sources and resources for your further investigation. You will also find downloads that accompany some of the activities I share, links to websites of some of the client case studies I mention, and more.

A Decision Only You Can Make

The number one factor that will determine your success has nothing to do with the breadth or depth of the material I cover in this book. If you work for yourself, you have what it takes to follow this system. The number one thing that determines whether you will succeed or fail with this system is something you can check off your list right now.

The question for you to answer is this: Will you decide to succeed?

You are smart enough. I will show you how to carve out enough time, so you will be able to build your business while still keeping your current life running. The next steps don't require significant investments and might even suggest you spend less time and money on activities you may be overinvesting in now.

This book offers you a quest: an adventure to win back your motivation, business, and life. All that's left for you to do is decide. Are you game to try the whole system? Or are you going to read this book for tips and tricks? You'll gain a ton of value either way. But the unstoppable success in business and life will be yours only if you commit to being all-in.

The first reveal is big: the neuroscience underpinnings of your success.

Phase I:

Coordinates of Your Current Location

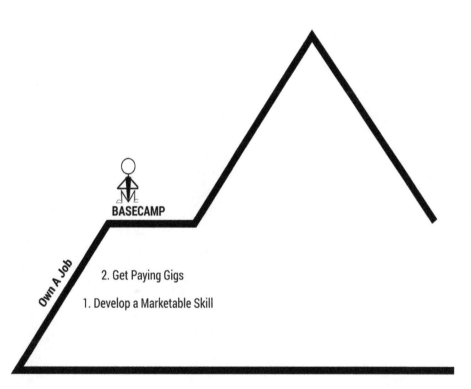

BASECAMP

Own A Job

2. Get Paying Gigs

1. Develop a Marketable Skill

CHAPTER 4:

Your Brain and Your Current Reality

During my master's, I decided to research the neuroscience behind why goals work. I did this because when I rebuilt my life, I believed everything started with a goal. (I later learned goals should come second.) Self-help is about setting goals; executive coaching is about goals; team performance is about shared goals; and operational efficiency consulting is about streamlining projects—which all started with goals.

What I discovered during my research went way beyond what I anticipated. I learned about a critical mechanism in our brains that explained why I was satisfied in some areas of my life and not others. I discovered that I was unknowingly responsible, the architect of everything—successful and not—in my life. Critically, I finally understood how to take control of my life and succeed at anything I wanted, even in areas where I had previously struggled.

What I teach you in this chapter is the single most important discovery I have made about success. It's a keystone piece of information that holds everything else together, and as luck would have it, I learned it by accident. What you learn about your brain in this chapter goes beyond helping you understand where you are now. It is the key to everything else you will learn in this book and beyond. You will discover how you came to arrive at this moment, having achieved some goals but not others, and how to retrain your brain to start achieving all of them.

I'll walk you through:

- The brain science behind what you have and have not achieved to date
- Two major ways you unknowingly program your brain to keep you from some of your goals and lead you instead to results you don't want
- The single most important success habit discovered by science and a guaranteed way to develop it

Your Subconscious and Your Success

When I first looked for research on the neuroscientific explanations of why goals work, I came up empty-handed. I later learned this was because the neuroscience of goals was a fledgling area of research. Fortunately, a friend put me in touch with a neuroscientist, Wil Cunningham, who specializes in the area of goal cognition and the brain. He directed me to some of the latest and most exciting research in his field, which answered my questions and more.

Wil started our conversation with the following activity. This activity requires you to close your eyes. To get the best results, take this book and move to a place where you can stand or sit facing a blank wall, a place where you can see nothing in your peripheral vision. Once you're in position, read the next step.

Activity: Facing a Blank Wall

In a moment, you will close your eyes and think of everything in your current surroundings, behind or around you, that is blue. This might include blue in an object on a table, a rug on the floor, or a piece of furniture. If you are in a room you know well, the blue might be something on a bookshelf, in a picture on the wall, or outside a window. When you believe you've inventoried all the blue, open your eyes. Please go ahead and close your eyes now and do this activity.

Debrief: Proceed After Completing the Steps Above

Eyes open? How'd you do?

I'm going to guess that you didn't recall all the blue in the room. It's extremely rare for anyone to capture one hundred percent of the blue around them. Many people even laugh a little because sometimes they realize they missed something obvious, such as a blue pen on their desk, something blue in a picture that's been hanging on the wall for years, or even something blue they are wearing.

Why Didn't You See All the Blue?

What Wil explained to me is there is too much information in our surroundings for us to notice it all. There are trillions of photons—elementary particles of light that contain information about our environment—and our conscious brains simply can't process them all. That's where your subconscious brain steps in. There is a region of your subconscious brain whose job it is to be on alert about your surroundings and to show you only those things it decides you need to see.

If you didn't recall all the blue, it's because your subconscious brain didn't think blue was all that important to you. For cognitive economy, "all the blue" didn't make the cut in the pre-filtering of your environment. But determining what you see is just the tip of the iceberg for your subconscious. Neuroscience has demonstrated that this subconscious pre-filtering process affects what you say and do, too. Even though it may feel like we are consciously in control of our lives, it turns out we aren't.

What feels like decisions about what we see, say, and do are pre-determined orders from our subconscious brains. What's more, neuroscientists have found that our subconscious brains are doing this filtering and deciding what we see, say, and do up to ten seconds before our conscious brains even become aware of what's going to happen.

Ten Seconds Behind

Up to a ten-second lag time was my wake-up call. When I learned this, I stopped in my tracks. I had heard of the reticular activating system and was familiar with the idea that my subconscious beliefs determined my behavior and success. Somehow, the idea that all this was happening up to ten seconds before my conscious mind even knew it was shocking.

For the first time, I understood that my subconscious had near-total control of my day-to-day existence, and subsequently, everything I had or hadn't achieved to date. That my conscious mind might be as much as ten seconds behind me in any given moment of my life.

I encourage you to stop reading right now, find a clock or timer with a second hand, and watch as ten seconds pass. Ten seconds. That's a *long* time for the conscious part of your brain to be on a need-to-know basis about what you will see, say, and do in any given situation. Too long to ignore.

The gravity of this insight felt more like an implosion than a light bulb moment. I am a believer in the idea that what you get in your life is a result of your actions. Here I was, struggling to achieve some of my most important goals, and I wasn't in conscious control of my actions: what I was seeing, saying, or doing at any given moment of my life.

Your Subconscious Decides What You See

When I continued digging into the research Wil directed me to, I began thinking about examples from my life. I realized I could identify countless examples of my subconscious brain calling the shots in the actions I took.

For starters, beyond not noticing all the blue, I could easily find examples of when I failed to see obvious things around me. Have you ever been with someone and they point out something interesting right in front of you? Something you didn't notice? Or how about that phenomenon of starting to see things once they become somehow relevant to you—for example, when you get a new car and notice that make of car everywhere? Two years ago, I got a dog. All of a sudden, my neighborhood was full of dogs. Of course, the dog population hadn't suddenly quadrupled; it was that my subconscious brain was tuned in to dogs and started showing them to me.

Your Subconscious Decides What You Say and Do

Then I noticed examples of times where I didn't feel in control of what I was saying. You know those times when you question what you are saying as you're saying it? When you wonder to yourself, "Why am I saying this? This is not going to go over well. I'm going to pay for this." But even as you were speaking the words and thinking that you'd regret them, you couldn't seem to stop yourself and said them anyway. Where did those words come from? Certainly not your conscious brain.

All of us have experienced our subconscious brain in control of what we are doing as we arrive somewhere familiar by car or on foot and realize we have no memory of traveling there. Once again, that's your subconscious loyally running the show for you.

Meet My Mom's Pony, Chiefy

My mom grew up rurally in Connecticut. Her family had an artesian well, a vegetable garden, and chickens. They also had an opinionated pony named Chiefy. In the summers, his job was to pull the cart so the children could distribute fresh eggs, vegetables, and water to nearby customers. He would pull up to each house along the route, stop, wait for the children to unload, then continue to the next house. After a reasonable amount of time at each stop, he would move on, regardless of whether the children were ready. Sometimes, they would have to run to catch up.

One day, after gearing up Chiefy, my mom and her siblings were called away. Hours later, Officer Clancy, a local policeman, arrived at their door with their pony in tow. Even with no one to take him out, Chiefy still followed his route. Fortunately, he liked Officer Clancy, who was able to lead the wayward pony back home.

This is how my mom's family came to call not paying attention to where you were going and ending up on a familiar route the "Chiefy route." It was synonymous with absent-mindedness. As I learned how the subconscious operated, I realized our Chiefy routes aren't absent-minded at all; they are other-minded. Our subconscious works similarly to an opinionated pony.

I contemplated, "If my conscious brain isn't even involved until my subconscious has made a decision, then what criteria is my subconscious using to make these decisions?" I hope you're wondering this, too, because it's a life-altering question, and knowing its answer will enable you to achieve immeasurably more of anything you want from now on.

The Misunderstood Amygdala

For years, your amygdala has been identified as the fear center of your brain. It's the part of your brain that stays on the constant lookout for danger in your environment and responds to any perceived threats by triggering the fight, flight, or freeze response. Your amygdala sometimes gets a bum rap for this because when it responds to perceived threats in your environment, it releases cortisol and other stress hormones that are not good for your health.

However, it turns out that this is not the full story of your amygdala. Recent neuroscience has found that your amygdala is also the region of your brain that prompts positive actions in response to environmental stimuli.

How does your amygdala decide how you will respond to environmental triggers? Its decisions are based on a type of goal that a team of neuroscientists led by Randall O'Reilly termed "hot goals." Hot goals are the goals your amygdala uses to determine everything you see, say, and do in response to your environment (and, therefore, everything you achieve).

There are two types of hot goals that your amygdala is tuned into: prevention and promotion goals. Prevention goals keep you from harm. Promotion goals make your life better. We are biologically wired to preserve life, so your amygdala pretty much knows what to do as far as prevention goals are concerned.

It's not as straightforward when it comes to your promotion goals. The main biologically-wired promotion goal is procreation. Your amygdala is happy to help you to achieve many other things that would make your life better. It would be glad to help you build an incredible business, make lots of money, be fit and healthy—but your amygdala doesn't come preloaded with those kinds of hot goals.

Conscious Goals Versus Subconscious/Hot Goals

Unfortunately, if you have a goal for yourself in your conscious mind, it doesn't automatically become a hot goal for your amygdala in your subconscious mind. That's because your conscious and your subconscious mind use different forms of language. (We will explore that in a moment.)

You can quickly determine which of your conscious goals are hot goals; they are the goals you automatically make progress on without needing to force yourself or draw on willpower. Wherever you are happy with the results you are getting in your life—such as your relationships, health, or how you spend your free time—your conscious goals are also hot goals.

Conversely, the goals that you've set for yourself time and time again but aren't speeding toward—like those New Year's resolutions you revisit year after year—are not hot goals and are unknown to your amygdala. Wherever you are frustrated or not making progress toward a goal you've consciously established for yourself, it's because what you consciously want your subconscious is unaware of; it is not a hot goal.

A conscious goal I have that is not also a hot goal is to visit Ireland. I've talked about going to Ireland for years but never have. When I learned about hot goals, I applied this information to my long-standing bucket-list trip to connect with a part of my heritage. I started looking at the excuses I make each passing year, and it became apparent to me what my actual hot goals were.

I live in Toronto, which is pretty cold and snowy in the winter. One of my conscious (and hot) goals is to be somewhere warm in the winter when I typically travel for months at a time. Ireland is cold in the winter so it never makes my list at that time of year. I could always visit Ireland in the summer, but I love staying close to home in the summer. I like to sail and spend time in nearby cottage country. I'm not keen on spending my vacation dollars when I'm happy to be at home. Despite my repeated thoughts about going to Ireland, it's just not a hot goal.

To figure out what's hot and what's not, simply take a look at your life. Where you feel your life is going well is where your conscious and subconscious (hot) goals are aligned. Wherever you're frustrated, your subconscious is not aware of what you want. Frustration is a function of your conscious mind; you can think of your subconscious as satisfied with everything about your life as it is now.

Who's in Charge?

If the bad news is that you don't have active control of your day-to-day actions and your subconscious is happy with the status quo that is your current life, the great news is that your conscious mind is in charge; it programs your amygdala. If there are things you want that you aren't automatically working toward, all you have to do to get going is program your amygdala.

You can think of your conscious mind like a computer programmer and your subconscious like a computer program. Your conscious mind programs your subconscious, but once it does, the program will run as written without judgments. Of course, sometimes computer programmers discover that there is a bug and their program isn't running the way they want it to. They can't just squeeze their eyes shut and hope that the computer program will change. No, the buggy program will continue to run until they sit down, debug, and reprogram it. The same is true for your brain; your subconscious will continue to run your life according to your hot goals whether or not you want them, but you can take charge and reprogram them.

The hitch, as I mentioned above, is that the conscious and subconscious parts of your brain don't speak the same language. Merely thinking about what you want won't get your subconscious aligned. Like a computer programmer needs a programming language to write software, you need to learn the language of your subconscious to rewrite your hot goals.

Two Languages

The language of your conscious brain is words, ideas, and concepts. It's the part of your brain that you use to make meaning of your world. The language of your subconscious brain is your senses—your sight, hearing, touch, taste, and smell—and your emotions. It's the part of your brain that you use to navigate and experience your world.

This is why just thinking about a concept or using words to describe a goal you have is not enough to create a hot goal. Your subconscious brain doesn't understand words, ideas, and concepts. To program a hot goal, you need to evoke your senses and emotions because that's what your subconscious will understand. Fear is a strong emotion. If you were bitten by a dog as a child and you see a dog now, your subconscious will access that fear and trigger your body to automatically cross the street or move away. To reprogram such a response, you would have to have real or imagined experiences with dogs that evoke feelings of safety. The more positive the feelings you manage to evoke while having these real or imagined encounters, the faster you would be able to reprogram your hot goal of fearing dogs.

If you're a student of success, I'm guessing the language of your subconscious doesn't surprise you at all. This is not the first time you've heard that you must imagine your success upfront and connect to how you will feel when you succeed. However, this might be the first time you've been made aware that your subconscious does not understand concepts and words.

If you've tried imagining success upfront, and it hasn't resulted in you naturally working toward your goals, the trick is in learning to "speak" to your subconscious in a way that your subconscious "hears" you.

Always Programming

Unlike a computer programmer who sits down, writes the programming, and then it's done, our conscious minds are constantly programming our subconscious minds. Mostly, this happens haphazardly, whether or not we're paying attention.

Every time you evoke your senses or emotions, you are programming hot goals you may or may not want. There are two main ways we haphazardly program our subconscious brains for things that we don't want. The first is when we accept messages from the outside world about ourselves and take those on as truths. The second is when we make a vow after an experience to which we react with emotional intensity.

Haphazard Programming Type I: Accepting Outside Messaging

I mentioned earlier that I am dyslexic. When I was in second grade, I had a teacher who couldn't deal with the differences in how I learned. She'd give class assignments, and I would do them backward. My letters were backward. My words were backward. I'd start at the back of the book and work to the front. Instead of her saying, "Oh, how interesting. You've done the right work, only backward. I wonder what's going on?" she told me I was stupid. She made me sit in the corner to punish me.

Although my mother arranged for me to change schools and get extensive remedial help all through my school career, there was never any consequence if I brought home a bad report card nor any expectation I might bring home a good one. Throughout my school career, feelings of inadequacy would well up in me whenever there was a graded assignment test or a report card issued. It was particularly painful because I was the youngest of four children, and my three siblings were each remarkable in unique ways.

Over the years, repeated messaging that my poor grades were to be expected juxtaposed the encouragement my siblings received to develop their talents. I came to believe I was somehow less than other people. Growing up was painful for me, and I became a recluse, depressed with low prospects for my future. Fortunately, my mom, who was trained in early childhood education and consequently worried about my low self-opinion, primed me with the idea that eventually became a hot goal: people who struggle in school can be great in business and life.

Hot Goals Running in the Background

Understanding what I now do about hot goals, my hindsight became 20/20. My mother's wise decision to implant the idea that I would be good at business and life had become a hot goal that led to me persistently developing my business knowledge. I believe it is also the hot goal that explains why I relentlessly pursued finding a vocation aligned to my purpose.

When I first started teaching online, I had to face another hot goal from my childhood. Teaching online requires exposure. I would have to put my thoughts, ideas, heart, and soul onto the Internet for all to see. My consulting business allowed me to work with leaders one-on-one or in small, controlled groups. It was a safe environment for my fears and insecurities. Despite having taught groups as large as fifty people for years, I struggled to bring myself to transition to online teaching.

The hot goal that blocked me had to do with my grade two teacher who ridiculed me in front of the classroom when I showed her my work-book. At only seven years old, I had begun programming a hot goal to hide my work.

What Repeated Messages Affected You?

Wherever you have struggled to make progress on a goal, there is a chance repeated messaging about what you are or are not good at is at the root. It may be a story like mine about you having a limited capacity in some way or another, or it may just be general stories that you heard about what it's like to work for yourself or run a business.

There is also the phenomenon of collective messaging that leads to the formation of hot goals, ideas that are not necessarily directed at you specifically, but that are so pervasive that you adopt them. Every solo business owner I've ever worked with has struggled with limiting hot goals regarding money. These are goals you've adopted through life that put limits on you or hold you back from achieving past a specific level.

Much of the middle-class mindset is about working hard. Messages that say that the harder we work the luckier we should get become hot goals that hold many people back from reaching their potential. Successful business owners will often tell you that making more money is easier than making less money. If you have a hot goal that running a business should be hard, your subconscious will not allow you to discover easier ways.

Haphazard Programming Type II: Making Vows

I certainly had a limiting hot goal around money. Mine was established in the second way we develop hot goals; I made a vow.

For the longest time, I wondered why I was able to help clients make six-, seven-, and eight-figure gains in their business while my business was stuck in the six-figure range. When I started looking for the hot goals that might be holding me back, I ended up discovering one I had made when I was thirteen years old.

My grandmother was sick; she was in the hospital for a long time, and I would hear my parents talking about how she was being cared for. Then came the day my grandmother died. We were all incredibly sad. My mother and father, stricken with grief, wondered about whether or not my relatives had done enough to get her the best medical care. At the time, my thirteen-year-old brain made the decision that my relatives did not get my grandmother the care they could have and so caused her death. At that point, I believed the only reason they might have done this was that they wanted her inheritance. Let's be clear: these were all only ideas in my childish imagination. My relatives are lovely people. But at thirteen, I made up creative stories and concluded that if you have money, people will kill you for it.

I remember telling myself I never wanted to have so much money that someone would kill me for it. Yikes. Fortunately, as I reflected on the disparate results I was able to create for other business owners and not myself, I figured there must be a hot goal at the root. Sure enough, when

I investigated what was going on, I remembered the long-forgotten (consciously—but not to my amygdala) story about my grandmother and the promise I made to myself.

Hot Goals Get Hotter with Time

Richard came to me for help leveling up his business. Despite being a rising star in his twenties and thirties, having made great money, and owning a home in one of the most expensive cities in the world, when I met Richard, he'd lost most of what he had built.

Richard was a software developer. His work was interesting enough, and his client base was meeting his needs. But he wanted to work on something he was more passionate about, so he gave up his client base to pursue a new tech start-up with a friend.

Early on, their new venture seemed to be off to the races. A big-name company agreed to partner with them once they'd built out their solution. The company made a small investment in them, but the lion's share of the money they needed for their development work came from family and friends and a second mortgage on Richard's home.

Richard and his partner spent three years on their venture. They had invested over $240,000 when their prospective partner was bought out by another company, which they discovered rendered their original agreement null and void. Lawyers advised them not to sue—they could end up spending more on legal fees than the money they'd lost.

Richard lost both his house in Toronto and his nerve. He walked out on his friend, leaving him with what remained of their start-up. He ended up going back to software development contract work. Unfortunately, in his time away, the market was flooded with new talent. As a result, Richard found himself making considerably less than he'd made before.

Richard's Limiting Hot Goal

When I learned Richard's story, I was confident he had hot goals that were limiting him. Hot goals have a way of becoming more evident in people's lives as they age, and Richard was in his late forties, a prime time for insidious hot goals to surface. One thing that stood out to me was that Richard had simply walked away from the business he'd created and helped develop. Surely, I thought, with all the time and effort invested, they could find another company willing to partner with them.

But things don't have to make sense when it comes to hot goals. I had a hunch Richard had a hot goal about exiting difficult situations. When we looked back at Richard's past, he recalled a bully who made life at school hard for him. The bully was a few years older and much larger than Richard. Richard's safety strategy at the time was to avoid encounters with the bully and to escape any encounters he did have as quickly as he could.

As a fourteen-year-old, it's probably a pretty good idea to quickly exit a situation in which you're threatened by a bully. Unfortunately, the subconscious locks in on hot goals for life until they are reprogrammed and does not differentiate between a threat from a bully you faced when you were a fourteen-year-old and a bully corporation you're facing in your forties. To your subconscious, a bully threat is a bully threat. If you have a hot goal about exiting difficult situations when faced with a bully, that's what you'll do—exit quickly.

As Richard and I worked through the activities that you will learn in this book, he was able to reprogram that hot goal that had been holding him back. We also found Richard's purpose, which in turn gave him the confidence he needed to start a new project. By using the system in this book, Richard is approaching his new opportunity more cautiously and keeping his current income coming in until there is clear evidence he can transition to his new business full time. Had Richard not discovered that hot goal, he would have continued to exit situations that felt bigger than him, putting him at risk of leaving any new business before reaching the exploitation phase. Richard is excited about life again and is on his way to building a business that's right for him.

A specific hot goal can work for or against you at any given time. As with Richard, when he was a young boy, it was not a bad course of action for him to quickly exit situations where he was sure to get pummeled. Yet as Richard matured and could defend himself, it was unwise of him to turn his back prematurely on a marketable venture in which he'd invested two years of his life and savings.

The Plus Side of Haphazard Programming

Whether through repeated messaging, cultural conditioning, or a vow you made in your past, your conscious mind is programming subconscious hot goals whenever you happen to trigger the language of senses and emotions that your subconscious understands.

Haphazard programming works in your favor whenever you imagine, sense, or emotionally react to good things happening to you, perhaps recognition you received or a time you did well at something you care about like sports, a hobby, an assignment at school or work, or positive experiences with friends.

Whenever you experience good things happening to you through your senses (such as your sight, hearing, or touch), and feel positive emotions (such as joy, delight, or gratitude), you are programming hot goals that will lead to more good things happening to you.

The hot-goal programming process works equally well when you *imagine* good things happening to you. This is because your subconscious can't tell the difference between things that are real and imagined. You might imagine being recognized for a skill or talent that others appreciate. You might visualize yourself living out your perfect day. You might see yourself laughing, smiling, and enjoying time with special people in your life.

Your Subconscious is Always Listening

Your subconscious is always being programmed when you happen to speak its language of senses and emotions. It doesn't matter whether the topic is past, present, or future. Your subconscious is always listening and forming or fortifying hot goals.

Good or bad, your subconscious does not judge your thoughts and feelings; it accepts your inputs at face value as a computer would. The more times you experience thoughts, images, senses, and emotions as they relate to a topic, the stronger your corresponding beneficial or limiting hot goal will become. Sudden emotional impacts like vows can speed up the process.

If you are worried because you have a lot of fear-based thoughts, hang tight. I'm going to teach you how you can reprogram limiting hot goals. But if you're not already, I encourage you to think of the bright side. All this time, you've been getting what you've been asking for, which is pretty cool if you stop and think about it. It means that if you want to get new things, you just need to learn how to get better at asking for what you want. Neuroplasticity means our brains are adaptable and will respond to new inputs.

Now that you are aware of subconscious hot goals and have a greater understanding of the role your hot goals play in the actions you take and the success you have achieved to date, the question becomes, what kind of relationship do you want to have with this part of your brain?

What Kind of Relationship Do You Want?

When I teach clients about hot goals, there is often an initial worry that their subconscious is trying to sabotage them with negative and limiting thoughts. I've heard people talk about the subconscious like it's a monkey brain or lizard brain that you need to try to control or overpower. I disagree. If you criticize this part of your brain, you're effectively telling a younger-version you (who established your hot goals) that you're wrong. We all know two wrongs don't make a right, and it's no different for you and your brain.

If anything, perhaps be humbled and grateful for a part of your brain that is so loyal that it will hold onto any instruction it's been given for life. And even though it might take some effort to reprogram your subconscious when up against past programming, when you do succeed, your amygdala is going to be equally loyal, automatically having you take actions toward whatever new hot goals you program. You've inadvertently put ideas in your subconscious as situations and experiences unfolded throughout your life. I encourage you to say no to hostility and yes to the beginning of a constructive and empowering new friendship.

I like to think of the conscious part of our brain as our chief executive officer (CEO) and our amygdala as the world's greatest assistant, which I call our chief time officer (CTO). Like in business, while a CEO may make the decisions, it's the rest of the team that needs to execute the CEO's plans; their initiatives won't get far without buy-in and execution from the rest of the team.

This is what it's like for your brain. Once you make a conscious decision, if you succeed at programming that decision as a hot goal, then your CTO will take responsibility for execution. It's pretty cool when you think about it. Your CTO automates you seeing, saying, and doing things that move you in the direction of your (hot) goals. When you understand how to harness the power of your CTO, and take the time to program it for what you want, becoming unstoppable is inevitable.

Naming Your CTO

At the beginning of your new relationship, you and your CTO might be on different pages. Be prepared for your new relationship to start awkwardly. After all, you want certain things, but your CTO may not be working toward those things. Right off the bat, there may be conflict. It will help to remind yourself that it was you who (even if inadvertently) provided instructions for any limiting hot goals in the first place.

To make this relationship work, you need to listen to your CTO, even when you don't like what it's saying. If it tells you, "You're too old for a new business venture," or "No one in your family is financially successful; what makes you think you will be?" you simply thank your CTO, then politely disregard it and do what you need to do. You're going to need to be able to listen to ideas from your CTO but not take them seriously or to try to fight them. Arguing with your CTO will be about as effective as trying to convince someone to switch allegiance from a favorite sports team or lifelong political party. It won't happen. There's a certain amount of respect, but there's also the awareness that you can have different ideas.

Have you ever seen an *Avengers* movie? With superheroes like the Avengers, it's rarely love and cooperation at first sight. *Au contraire.* They start as fighting foes, vying for status and recognition. Along the way, they discover they have the same goals and common enemies and become comrades who are invincible when together. I've overseen the forming of many CEO/CTO relationships, and that's what this journey can look like for you. It's incredible to witness.

One way to jump-start your relationship and speed up your reprogramming efforts is to give your CTO a name. Just calling it "subconscious" or "amygdala" is too impersonal. You want a name that makes your conscious brain comfortable enough to disagree with your CTO without inspiring anger and argument. Since you'll be using this name for the rest of your life, I find it best to have fun with it, as my group program participants do. In the group I taught before writing this book, we had CTOs named Pinky, Lance, Karen, Peewee, and Von Trapp. My CTO is Samantha.

Remember earlier in this book when I offered a fair warning that we'd be working at the power station, not the light switch level anymore, and if you proceeded there would be no turning back? Your CTO represents your power station, and if you decide to name yours, from this day forward, you'll be regularly talking to yourself (not necessarily out loud). It's going to be the two of you taking on the world as a team from now on!

Good Relationships Take Time

What if your CTO doesn't immediately react to your new instructions? You're not only stuck with your CTO, but you share a face, so you can't throw a punch like an Avenger and expect anything good to happen. Your best option is to realize that reprogramming old hot goals takes time. Practicing a combination self-compassion and perseverance will set you up for success. Keep in mind that when things aren't going your way, a younger version of you (who felt the need to stay safe) programmed your CTO to take the actions that have led to the results you're getting now.

It's not your CTO's fault. Your CTO is your younger self's messenger. No amount of anger at younger you for feeling unsafe or afraid, and no amount of shooting the messenger, will get you anywhere constructive. Instead, anger and frustration on your part will only delay how long it takes you to reprogram your CTO. A loving, compassionate, yet firm approach is the most efficient way to turn such a situation around.

The older you are or the more entrenched an old hot goal is, the more you can anticipate your CTO's sneaky resistance. Sneaky resistance from your CTO will come in the form of convincing thoughts that cite external reasons, such as market conditions or other people's actions, are to blame for falling short of your goals. Your CTO might also trigger self-deprecating thoughts—ideas that you're not good enough, and the problem is you. Either way, while these thoughts may seem valid, they are not. These are automated thoughts triggered by old hot goals.

As you develop your new relationship with your CTO, I encourage you to maintain a constructive attitude and positive expectations for how things will work out. You are where you are. Any situation can be turned around. As William Shakespeare said, "Things are neither good nor bad, but thinking makes it so." Hold faith that you will onboard your CTO and together make the best of your circumstances, and you will.

Easing into Your New Relationship

Here are three relationship-building practices to help you get off on the right foot with your CTO.

Practice I: Demonstrate Your Independence

Despite your subconscious determining most of what you see, say, and do at any given moment in time, you can consciously take control of your actions when needed. You don't want to live your whole life taking conscious control, because it would be exhausting (and impossible), but it's important to know that you are able to take conscious control of your decisions and actions when you put your mind to it.

A practice that will help demonstrate your independence is to walk around as you say, "I'm not walking around." You can do this with anything: Say you're not making dinner while you make dinner, or that you're not petting the dog while you pet it. What this activity does is demonstrate that you can (temporarily) disobey your subconscious, if and when needed.

Practice II: Rise Above Disappointments

Life comes with its share of disappointments. To reach your next level of success will require you to respond differently to disappointing circumstances and events. Many people have hot goals that cause them to exaggerate the magnitude of disappointing events. They would tell you they are realistic, but focusing on negatives is pessimism. A pessimistic outlook is dangerous because it inhibits your ability to see pragmatic solutions and opportunities.

If you are predisposed to thinking pessimistically, do not worry. That is just your CTO's former programming from former events in your life, and it's well within your power to reprogram yourself to make the best of disappointing situations. From now on, whenever you encounter a (or think of a past) disappointing event, ask yourself, "How can I take this situation and turn it into the best thing that could have happened?"

You might read this and think I'm trying to sneak in ideas around optimism. You're right. But a lot of people don't understand what optimism is. Optimism is not about being delusional. Optimism is about being realistic about what's happening and making the best of your circumstances. Making the best of your circumstances is just a smart thing to do.

Practice III: Become a Curious Investigator

Another practice that will support you when you experience disappointments and setbacks is to avoid judging yourself or others and focus instead on what lesson you can learn or what hot goals might be running in the background.

If you've learned about meditation, have been introduced to Cognitive Behavioral Therapy (CBT), or have read just about any book on healing emotions, you've been introduced to the idea of no judgment. You'll be gaining tools throughout this book to help you build a positive, no-judgment relationship with your CTO. For now, when thinking of old or current situations that have upset you, do your best to stay neutral and curious about your lessons or underlying hot goals.

Depending on how old you are, there will be more or less to unwind and reprogram. But it's doable. I've discovered and reprogrammed dozens of limiting hot goals; our Ignite and Basecamp participants have, and my nearly eighty-year-old mom has too. It may take longer than you want to discover and reprogram your hot goals, but if you stick with it, your success is a matter of time.

What Hot Goals Are Limiting You?

You may be wondering what unwanted hot goals have been holding you back. Use this activity to discover the origin of unwanted hot goals and how they've been limiting you.

Investigate: Looking back on your past, consider repeated negative messages or limiting vows around work. Did you hear things like, "It's hard to be in business for yourself?" Were you told you were lazy or not smart? That it's safer to work for someone else than it is to work for yourself? That people who work hard are good and rich people are bad?

Make the Connection: After you've written down limiting ideas that you have heard about success and self-employment, take some time to consider each of them and how each has affected your behavior, decisions, and results to this point in your business and life.

Express Gratitude: This may feel counterintuitive, but what you don't know you can't address. Be grateful every time you discover a hot goal that isn't working for you; each one you discover introduces an opportunity to program a new hot goal to achieve whatever you want.

Decide: For each hot goal that isn't working for you, put your hand on your heart and say aloud, "This hot goal came from my past. This hot goal doesn't work for me anymore and is not keeping me safe. I will reprogram my CTO, [insert name], for [insert what you want] from now on."

Accessing Your Power Station

Learning my subconscious decides most of my actions up to ten seconds in advance of my conscious awareness has enabled me to take control of important facets of my life. Once I understood the mechanisms through which my brain and body operate, I went from grasping at straws, winning some goals and losing others (and having no idea why), and constantly feeling like a pawn in the universe to understanding the power I had to change anything.

The relationship between my conscious mind and subconscious was consistent with everything I had ever heard before but was more powerful when I understood the science of what was going on. I stopped looking to the law of attraction and the universe to solve my problems and make my dreams come true. I started focusing on reprogramming my brain to take automatic action (although I never turn down help from the universe either).

Your subconscious is the command and control center for what you see, say, and do—the power station of how you spend your time. It wants to keep you safe and instinctively behaves in ways it thinks it can accomplish that. Your subconscious wants to help you thrive, but it doesn't necessarily know what that means. You have to tell it.

Everything we do from here on out in this book will involve reprogramming your CTO. The techniques I offer you for each step of this system are designed with the idea of translating what you want into a language your CTO can hear.

When you program hot goals, anything you want becomes possible. If you are clear on what you want, then consider yourself fortunate. If, on the other hand, you're like most of our Basecamp clients, then you're probably not crystal clear on the business you want to build. The dilemma is that you must be both passionate and precise about your goals if you're going to program hot goals. Discovering your purpose, clarifying your vision, and selecting new value-based behaviors—a trio of outcomes I call your Happiness Recipe—make it far easier to choose goals you'll be passionate about pursuing.

CHAPTER 5:

Your Happiness Recipe

D o you know the movie *Ready Player One*? It's a sci-fi film about a future world in which most human interaction occurs within a virtual reality setting. The virtual realm's eccentric creator dies, leaving the kingdom's keys to whoever can complete his quest. It's an epic contest with dozens competing fiercely for the prize, but the secret to prevailing is not to be found out there where everyone rushes to look but requires taking a journey within.

When it comes to figuring out our life purpose, determining our life goals, or choosing values to live by, many people do the same: we look "out there" to find answers we hope will lead us to a happier existence. We read books, watch talks, listen to podcasts, and travel, but what I learned in my decade-long quest for these answers was that like the movie *Ready Player One*, the answers about how to be happy were already within me, waiting to be discovered.

The Bottle-Neck was My Purpose

I had all but given up searching for my purpose when I discovered there was little chance of realizing my business dreams until I figured mine out. I was working on clarifying a business vision because during my master's, I found compelling research that entrepreneurs guided by a vision outperformed their peers on every major factor of performance by ten to twelve times. That was a motivating statistic, and since I was reinventing my business at such a late stage in my life, developing a vision became my top priority.

My challenge was this: The kinds of visions that delivered ten to twelve times benefits were always long term and underscored by the leader's purpose, and I had no confidence in mine. I'd tried to find my purpose for years and was even starting to question whether I would ever figure it out. Oh sure, I had an idea about what it might be. But did I have the level of unwavering confidence I needed to lock in on a business vision for the next ten or twenty years? No, I did not.

Fortunately, at the time I was struggling with the question of my purpose, I was introduced to Professor Elangovan (known as Elango), an inspiring faculty member at the University of Victoria whose area of study is helping leaders find their calling. Over a number of dinners, Elango taught me a way of thinking about purpose I had not understood before.

A New Path to Purpose

Through my discussions with Elango and field trials in the years afterward, I finally understood why so many people have difficulty finding their purpose. I was fortunate to have an opportunity to test and refine the method because, back then, I was running my first online group programs. Since I had just found my purpose, I offered my program participants the option of trying out the activities I'd learned from Elango to see if they might discover theirs, too.

The outcomes thrilled my clients. Not all the clients in my initial groups found their purpose on their first attempt, but they all found clues and a path that would eventually lead them to discover their purpose.

Over the years, I continued to refine the method and presented my group program clients with the same offer. "No promises, but let's give this purpose-finding process a try just in case it works." The rate of my clients' successes grew, as did my confidence with the method.

During these years, I discovered that there are widespread misconceptions about what our purpose should sound like, be like, and feel like, and most critically, what we need to do with our purpose once we've found it. With all these misconceptions in play, it's no wonder so many people struggle to figure out their purpose. Below, I address these misconceptions before sharing the process I now use with my clients and program participants.

Our Ignite and Basecamp participants often report this work feels like re-introducing themselves to themselves. And while it's nice to do activities that feel good, knowing your purpose is crucial to your success because your CTO pays attention to when you feel good. Remember, your CTO is on the lookout for promotion goals, things that make your life better; it just doesn't know what those things are unless you tell it through the language it understands. This language includes the beautiful feelings that using the purpose-finding process in this chapter will instinctively evoke.

What Is a Purpose?

When I Googled "purpose definition," the first search result was, "The reason for which something is done or created or for which something exists." I prefer happiness expert Richard Layard's simpler definition of purpose as "your reason for waking up in the morning." When I ask my clients and program participants what they think a purpose is, I get answers, such as, "It's what drives you," "It's your reason for being," "It's how you contribute," "It's a way to realize your potential and radiate joy," and "It's what gives your life meaning." All are fine definitions, yet none of them help you recognize when you've successfully discovered your purpose.

What my clients and I have found is that your purpose is something that makes you intrinsically happy when you do something connected to it or even simply think about it. The more you think about, choose, and engage in activities that are related to your purpose, the more motivated you feel each day. Over time, the more you link your thinking and doing to your purpose, the happier you become.

In its simplest terms, we're looking for what makes you intrinsically happy.

What Are You Expecting?

Another thing that holds people back from discovering their purpose is their expectation of what it will be like when they find theirs. Take a moment to consider what you're expecting it to be like when you discover yours. What do you expect it to feel like? What will take place? How will you know for certain it's your purpose?

When I ask my clients what they expect, they say things like, "It will be ecstatic and hopeful," "An enlightening moment," "Things will immediately feel effortless," "There will be freedom from all the small nonsense," and that they will "start radiating joy." Their responses echoed mine when I was searching and couldn't trust the answers I was getting.

Most people are expecting a dramatic "aha" moment with fanfare, confetti, and a marching band. After all, finding your meaning of life is an epic accomplishment most people never reach. But the reality is when your purpose finally appears, it's more like a whisper than a roar.

Here's What We Get Instead

I live in an area brimming with mature oak trees. It's quite beautiful, but it becomes downright dangerous each year in late summer and early autumn when I am pebbled with acorns. I think about acorns a lot for a few months each year. When I thought about purpose, I realized it was just like the acorn and the oak tree. It's highly unlikely anyone would look at an acorn for the first time and guess that it contains all the information needed to become an oak tree, but it does.

What's interesting about purpose is that it's not usually a big and splashy moment. There aren't typically fireworks or sudden realizations of the meaning of life. Instead, there's a small and fascinating idea, an acorn, that if you nurture, can become everything you hoped for and more. Like in nature, we don't get our purpose in the finished form of an oak tree. To realize the full majesty of our purpose, we need to start with a seed and nurture it.

When I first found my purpose acorn, I didn't trust it. But, like an acorn, it's grown in direct proportion to how often I nurtured it. I've been nurturing mine for several years now; as a result, it's come into focus. I have aligned everything about my business around it, and it fills me with joy every time I think about it. I've only been at this a few years, and I already feel incredible almost every day. I can hardly imagine how much better things will get as my sapling purpose continues to grow into a mighty oak purpose.

The takeaway is that the goal is to find your purpose acorn using the activities described below and then nurture it so it becomes a sapling and eventually a mighty oak.

What Your Purpose Will Sound Like

Purpose is commonly confused with the idea of a mission. Missions are meaningful projects such as digging a well or building a school, saving rainforests or the oceans, raising great kids, or even giving great customer service above and beyond others in your industry. The neat thing about your purpose is that it's not limiting like that. Your purpose can be expressed through many kinds of projects, and it doesn't limit you to a specific vocation.

Purpose is more liberating. It expands your options. It's a feeling that can be expressed and nurtured in a variety of ways. Here are purposes of some of the people I've worked with: increasing joy, beating expectations, nurturing growth, shining a light on beauty, raising the underdog, celebrating stories, making discoveries, being carefree.

In the past when I tried to discover my purpose, I thought my purpose might be "helping people achieve their potential." I've now come to realize it is "causing dreams to come true." Is helping dreams come true connected to the idea of helping people achieve their potential? Absolutely.

But it's a nuance that makes a difference and is far more motivating to me. As you can see, my purpose is not a limiting mission or vocation but rather something that I could achieve through many activities and professions.

I have decided to be a coach and educator in the field of business and high-performance because I happened to have a lot of experience in those areas, and there is a widespread need for people to learn how to build profitable businesses that enable a healthy quality of life. I could just as easily have been an elementary school teacher, a minister, a director, a mountain climbing instructor, or a piano teacher, and all of those activities would enable me to live my truth of causing dreams to come true.

Who Do You Do Your Purpose For?

Many people have come to me with preconceived notions about their purpose, which they have developed in business programs they've taken. A purpose from a business program might sound something like this: "I help people increase their confidence." On the surface, this sounds nice. But a purpose is not just something you do for other people, and it's not just something you do for yourself. It's something you want for everybody and, critically, always includes you.

One of my group program participants, Tony, discovered that his purpose is creating joy. Shortly afterward, he was at a holiday party with the assignment of nurturing his purpose by creating joy for the people in attendance. At one point, he noticed a man speaking to a woman and making her happy. For a brief moment, he felt annoyed, thinking, "Hey, that's my job." Moments later, Tony's emotions changed as he realized that man was assisting him with his job.

When you have found and start to nurture your purpose, you'll find it transcends business and competition. It's so much bigger than that. Keep in mind, your purpose isn't limited to a business play. It's a key to you feeling intrinsically happy and getting your CTO on board with your plans. It's something that you can't help but feel good about. Like Tony, once you find yours, you'll want it for everyone.

You may wonder about your "competition." For instance, how do I view the people in my space who also cause dreams to come true? I celebrate them. I wish them success. Why? Because every time I learn a dream has come true, whether I've had a hand in it or not, the joy I feel is palpable. When you have found and start to nurture your purpose, you won't want to be competitive about it. You'll want it for everyone and anyone. Methodically following the steps to explore before you exploit your business is how you compete—not by trying to hold a monopoly on your purpose.

A final word of caution. There is a tendency when you find your purpose to start wanting to do it for others. That's a wonderful instinct of service. But it's not where you start. The first thing I encourage you to do once you find your purpose acorn is to get busy bringing that expression into your life. You'll know when it's time to turn the focus to others; it's when the fire starts burning so brightly inside you that you can't possibly contain it.

Find Your Purpose Acorn

There are three phases to finding your purpose acorn. First, you are going to collect data by writing some stories. Second, you will analyze your stories to identify your purpose acorn contenders. Third, you will nurture your purpose acorn contenders to see which one resonates.

Step 1: Collect the Data

Look back on your life and think of the times when you were most proud of yourself. You will be looking for four to five stories (or more). I encourage you to look for stories at different ages and in different parts of your life. They could include stories from childhood, school, travels, work, parenthood, sports, clubs, associations, or communities. As you write your stories, consider these questions:

- What was the situation?
- What were you doing?
- What did you like or appreciate about the situation?

- What made the time special?
- What made you feel proud?

Take your time as you recall as many stories as possible and be open to what they might be. The stories that make us feel proud can run the gamut. I've heard stories ranging from shining shoes to visiting grandparents and going out for dim sum to wearing hand-me-downs at school. Here's an example from a Basecamp participant, Shawna Robins, founder of Kaia Health and the author of the best-selling book, *Powerful Sleep*.

Bear Spotting!

One of my most favorite places in this world is in Yosemite National Park, in a place called Tuolumne Meadows. We used to camp there for two weeks every year, and I looked forward to it. I could get away from the small, strict Catholic school (which I deeply hated); my parents yelled less and were more relaxed there; and I could be dirty and free and wander around with parents. It was bliss! Plus it is full of incredible natural beauty. One time, my father warned me to stay out of the forest path because someone had spotted a bear that morning. So when he went fishing, I snuck into the forest to look for a bear. I quietly hid behind some bushes and waited. I loved watching the afternoon light dance between the trees. The forest was cool and peaceful. The wildflowers swayed in the breeze. I felt such a deep sense of calm. I never did see the bear, but my father was very mad at me when I returned back to the camp. He knew I had disobeyed him. But I was so connected to the forest and its peace that I just smiled at him and admitted that I had disobeyed him, I understood my punishment, and I stayed in the tent for the rest of the day. That day was worth any punishment. It was like I found a piece of my soul that day. I felt whole.

I encourage you to take a few days and savor this step of the activity. When you have completed four or more stories, you can proceed to step two, theming your stories.

Step 2: Theme Your Stories

Once you've written four or more stories, the next step is to theme your stories. Theming starts with identifying main ideas within each story. Take Shawna's story, for example. There were several potential main ideas. Her story was about spending time with her parents. It was about spending time in nature. It was about *not* being at school, which she deeply hated, and it was about being determined to do things her way—even if there were consequences. From this one story alone, it would be difficult to figure out Shawna's purpose, as it could have been aligned with any of these main ideas. This is why you want to highlight as many main ideas in each of your stories before you try to guess what your purpose acorn might be.

After you have themed each of your stories individually, you progress to looking for the patterns, or repeated main ideas, across them. In Shawna's case, her other stories were about surprising her neighbors with bouquets of fresh cut flowers, adventure cycling at four years old, dancing and singing on roller skates by herself when girls in a new neighborhood wouldn't play with her, and studying abroad against the advice of family and friends. There was nothing on the surface that matched her adorable story of waiting for a bear. But when we compared the main ideas in each of her stories, two were present in each one: following her own path and adventure. This was our clue that her purpose was going to be close to one or both of these ideas.

The final step of theming is to pick a purpose acorn contender. To do this, look at the main ideas from your stories and identify which ideas are repeated in all of your stories. The ideas that are evident in all your stories are the clues to your purpose. From here, you identify a purpose acorn contender that feels like it could be right. You don't need to get your purpose acorn perfect on the first try because if you nurture a purpose contender for several weeks and the idea does not make you feel more and more inspired every time you think of it, you simply return to the stories you've written, reconsider the main ideas and pick another contender.

If you are struggling to do this independently, I urge you to get a second opinion. Make sure to ask someone who cares for your success and whose opinion you value. Share your stories with them and ask them to follow the same steps you did. Request that they identify the main ideas in each of your stories before trying to identify the themes among your stories. Even if you think you have found your purpose acorn, I highly recommend you take this step. When I work with my clients and program participants, they often have a hard time looking at their "data" with enough neutrality to see it clearly. A second opinion from someone you trust can lead to surprising revelations.

Step 3: Nurture Your Purpose Acorn Contender

Once you identify your purpose acorn contender, all you have to do to "nurture it" is find ways to connect your daily activities (including your business activities) to the idea you identified. When you wake up, think about your purpose and what you could do during the day ahead that would enable you to express it—much like Tony, who endeavors to add joy to as many situations as possible.

The more you do this, the clearer your purpose becomes. When I thought my purpose was helping people reach their potential, I frequently called that idea to mind when working with clients. As I paid attention to my inner feelings, I noticed I'd get deeply happy for my clients' wins and successes. In time, I realized my purpose was causing dreams to come true. Are the two ideas related? Sure. But helping someone reach their potential is an enormous proposition, and all I needed was to help dreams coming true—big and small—to feel intrinsically great.

When Shawna first themed her stories, she wrote, "I think my purpose is to push through adversity to find happiness." As Shawna nurtured her purpose, she realized her purpose is "helping others (and herself) experience adventure." Shawna discovered that adventure was her central theme because every time she thought of her past adventures, she got frisson, a tingling feeling in her body that told her she was on the right track.

Once we knew that the idea of adventure made Shawna intrinsically happy, we refocused her health coaching business to align with this idea. Shawna created a "wellness upgrade" program specifically for people who wanted better energy levels to live more fun (and adventurous) lives. To this end, Shawna created Irresistibly Healthy, a program for successful women who'd put their health on the side burner while raising their families or building their careers. Irresistibly Healthy energizes Shawna because it helps women gain the energy they need to have more adventures in their lives.

One thing to keep in mind as you use this process is to remember, like Shawna, when you first start thinking about what your purpose might be, you don't have to get it exactly right to experience positive results. Even finding an idea close to your purpose will point you in the right direction. You'll know when you discover the "purpose acorn" you resonate with most because when you do, your senses will light up whenever you think about it.

Your Purpose and Your CTO

Thinking about your purpose, or something close to it, helps you "speak" the language your CTO understands. When you think of your purpose, you trigger intrinsic positive emotions enabling your CTO to take note of new goals you associate with it. The more you deliberately call your purpose to mind, the more you will trigger a distinctive, intrinsically good feeling-signature, that will make it easier for you to program new hot goals.

Over time, as you align your projects and activities with your purpose acorn, something marvelous happens. You start feeling better and better about your life. Your CTO takes more actions that move you toward your goals. As it does, you feel increasingly intrinsically motivated. You stop waiting for someday to be happy; you feel better about your life as it is today.

If, after actively nurturing a purpose acorn for several weeks, you're not feeling increasingly intrinsically energized, then the likelihood is, you didn't find the right purpose acorn. The exciting part is you already have the data you need to find the right one. All you need to do is return to your stories and retheme them; as in *Ready Player One*, the clues are within.

When you've found your purpose, it will make you feel great every time you think of it. Your purpose becomes an important element of your vision—what you plan to accomplish down the road. The most motivating visions will be the result of years of nurturing your purpose. The most effective visions will be a future reflection of your purpose in action.

Your Vision for Your Future Happiness

Once you have identified your purpose, it's time to determine objectives for what you want to achieve in the years ahead. Establishing a meaningful, long-term objective for your business (or life) is known as "creating a vision." Google dictionary defines vision as "the ability to think about or plan the future with imagination or wisdom." You can create visions with varying timeframes, and the timeframe you choose can significantly impact your success.

Earlier in this chapter, I shared research that entrepreneurs with visions for their companies outperform their competition by a factor of ten to twelve. As with most things, success is in the details. A vision that will catapult you past your competition needs to be long term—at least ten or more years—underscored by your life purpose, and so motivating that you would never imagine changing it, no matter the circumstances. As you might imagine, locking in on such a vision is no small undertaking and a commitment you should not take lightly.

There's best-practice timing you'll want to follow when developing your vision. If you are struggling with what target market to focus on or what your product or services should be, now is not the right time for you to commit to ten-plus-year goals. A well-developed vision becomes an accelerant only once you feel fully committed to the track you've chosen.

Since the people who join Basecamp have yet to clarify their tar-get-market, signature programs, or business models, I have come to dis-cover that starting with three-year objectives—what I call a pathfinder-vi-sion—is an empowering place to start. A pathfinder vision requires you to articulate your ideal working day, three years from today.

As the name suggests, a pathfinder vision gets you moving in the right direction. Once you commit to a target market, positioning and prove your business model—which takes most of my clients about a year—you can circle back to establish a long-term vision.

Create Your Pathfinder Vision

To create your pathfinder-vision, imagine yourself three years from today, and that every area of your business is working as you want. Clients adore your products and services. Marketing and sales are easy, and you have the money and work/life balance you want. With this picture in your mind, imagine the particulars of your ideal workday from start to finish. Include details such as where you are, who you are with, and your various activities throughout the day. See yourself getting a new client or customer and how much you get paid and for which services/products. Imagine yourself delivering on promises to your clients and how happy they are with your work. Finish by journaling about your imagined experiences, including as many details as you can.

Repeat the pathfinder-vision visualization activity as many times as you need to until you are happy with what you are picturing for your ideal workday three years from now. With knowledge of what you want for three years from today clarified, you'll be able to make much better decisions about what to do with your business next.

Resist a Fame Driven Vision

A problem I've seen when people do their pathfinder visions is choosing inflated goals that aren't truly meaningful. For example, when imagining what they want, they choose things such as being celebrated by Oprah, having millions of social media followers, or making millions of dollars a month. In my experience, our clients who focus on providing real value to *their* clients build more profitable and exciting businesses than those who fantasize about becoming famous, building followings, or getting rich.

One of our clients, whom I'll call Elaine, initially had this problem. Elaine was an intuitive coach whose clients adored the results they got with her. She enrolled in Basecamp because she noticed that her clients often made considerable sums of money based on her guidance, yet she was living month-to-month, selling her time by the hour or, at best, package of hours. She was ready to create a serious business from her skills, which would finally protect her future.

When Elaine first did the pathfinder vision activity, she imagined herself as a famous intuitive who had become a household name worldwide. Not only was this a stretch for what's possible in three years, but nowhere in her journaling about her ideal working day did she articulate how she saw herself helping and serving others. Elaine had focused solely on being seen, recognized, and celebrated for her talents. When I asked her about this, she told me she thought helping others was implied and did not need to be articulated. But to have power over her CTO, she was wrong.

The problem with fame-driven goals is that your CTO is not likely to help you work on a goal unless it's truly meaningful. I've noticed that people in service-businesses who focus their visions on achieving fame and recognition tend to struggle for years. Conversely, those who focus on helping others for the sake of being of service tend to grow their businesses on shorter timelines.

Elaine had a big heart and wanted to help millions of people. When I pointed out her three-year goals were all about fame and missing specifics on whom she would help and how she planned to help them, Elaine saw the problem. What she cared about most was helping her clients, so she went back to the drawing board and redid her pathfinder vision activity. The second time around, her three-year vision was that she had created an in-demand signature experience, and it had become so popular, that she was working on ways to scale her reach. That was a realistic outcome for a three-year time frame, so it was a far better pathfinder vision.

Karate students must achieve an orange, blue, yellow, green, and brown belt before attempting their black belt. The same is true of business. When you right-size your goals for where you are now, you position yourself to advance predictably. Elaine might become a famous intuitive coach one day, but to expect that in just three years, before she's created a signature program, was unrealistic. By making her three-year goals ambitious but not improbable, Elaine has positioned herself for success.

Your Vision and Your CTO

Even when you right size your goals, it's not uncommon for self-doubt to creep in when you do your pathfinder vision activity. If thinking of your three-year goals has caused you to fret, please know that self doubt is normal and expected at the beginning of a journey to anywhere new. New achievements start with new goals, and fretting when you think of a goal is merely a sign that what you want now is different from hot goals you created in your past.

Many capable people get stuck in their businesses and lives because they misinterpret self-doubt as a sign that they can't reach a goal. Self-doubt is usually just a sign you want something that's in opposition to one or more of your outdated hot goals. The process you will learn in chapters seven through thirteen will help you program new hot goals; in the meantime, to calm your CTO, I suggest coming up with a few back-of-the-napkin ideas for achieving your pathfinder vision.

To do this, on the top of a clean page, write the average amount of money you imagined yourself earning per month in your pathfinder vision. Next, force yourself to come up with five to fifty ideas for how you could make this amount of money doing something you love. Pro tip: Include a few ideas for a signature program or proprietary process on your list. How many ideas do you need? As many as required to end up with two or three that seem fun and plausible to you.

Since you have a hot goal to do what you're doing now and earn the living you are earning now, you can expect your CTO to pipe up with a lot of, "No way! That idea is crazy. That's too much effort. That one? That is a terrible idea. No one will buy that from you." Remember to thank but not entertain your CTO ("I appreciate you pointing out that I have out-of-date hot goals, but I'm busy right now.") and then create your list of ideas anyway.

As you come up with ideas, hold faith that you will discover a purpose-aligned way to serve others and make the money you want. Keep telling yourself that there is an idea waiting for you that will be good for you and good for others but that you haven't been able to think of it (yet) because your CTO has been trying to keep you safe. Assure your CTO that serving others and earning the amount of money you identified will make you safe and persist in coming up with ideas until you arrive at two or three that have merit.

The outcome of this brainstorming session is to give you and your CTO some assurance that there are feasible ways for you to create the business and life you want. In my experience, there are always purpose-aligned ways to make money that you haven't considered. In the next chapter, you will learn more about the expertise business growth model and how to build a business that you can eventually grow or scale. First, we need to look at your Happiness Recipe's third and final element, introducing new value-based behaviors.

Choose New Values to Speed Up Success

You might be surprised to hear this, but your current values have everything to do with how successful your business is, how much money you make, and how happy you are. Unless you revisit your values, you can expect more of the same results you are currently getting as time passes. Google dictionary defines values as "a person's principles or standards of behavior; one's judgment of what is important in life." In other words, your values guide your day-to-day behaviors, which in turn, determine everything you will or won't achieve.

We've already discussed how your CTO is determining almost all of your day-to-day actions. Now it's time to introduce the idea that one of the ways your CTO is determining your day-to-day actions is based on your values, which, over the years, have become your hot goals. For the most part, we are not all that aware of the values we live by. Although we think we know what values we live by, our actions rarely line up with them as closely as we think. To discover this for yourself, try the following activity.

Step 1: Select Your Top Values
Take a moment and think of what you consider to be two or three of your top values and write them down on a piece of paper. If values do not come to mind immediately, put this book down now and give yourself a moment to think about some of the principles or standards of behavior you believe in most. When you have determined some of your top values, write them down and proceed to the next step.

Step 2: Rate Your Top Values
Now that you have identified some of your most cherished values, take a moment and think about the degree to which you currently adhere to each one. Rate yourself on a scale of one to ten, with one being "you don't honor that value at all" and ten being "there would be no way for you express that value more fully in the way you live."

Step 3: Debrief Your Ratings
If you are like the majority of the people I've done this activity with, then you probably surprised yourself as you rated your adherence to your top values between five and eight. Most people rate themselves a six or a seven, with only the rare person rating themselves a nine or a ten. This activity teaches us that your stated values are not necessarily a representation of who you are but rather ideals for who you want to be.

Ideals versus Values in Action
It is important to understand that oftentimes, our stated values are different than the values we live by in practice. For example, many people I work with espouse the value of honesty and then admit they don't always speak their mind. I also had one fellow who rated himself as a nine out of

ten on integrity, yet he was frequently late and wasn't very thorough with his assignments. Two behaviors which point to lower integrity.

When your stated values differ from the values you live by, you can be sure the ones you live by were inherited from your parents or social situations growing up. While most values sound like wonderful ideals (because all values tend to sound wonderful), keep in mind the ones you actually live by have gotten you to where you are now in life.

No matter how altruistic your stated values are, there is a small likelihood your current value set is optimized to help you achieve your goals. I know this because if your values were working for you, you'd be behaving in ways that would be accelerating you toward what you want. You'd be fast-tracking so quickly toward your goals that it would be obvious everything you want is on its way to you. Those values handed down from your upbringing may be inspirational, but they're probably not the values you need to focus on to get you the success you want.

Since—as the saying goes—doing what you've always done leads to getting the results you've always gotten, you will want to identify new values to live by if you want to achieve something new. No matter how idealistic your top values-in-practice are, they are not likely to be the ones you will need to focus on to upgrade your situation. Choosing empowering new values will help you fast track your success. Fortunately, the values that will empower us are easy to identify.

Identify Empowering Values

Most people do value updates wrong. They come up with a few ideas that sound and feel meaningful to them, write them down, and then fail to follow through with the hard work necessary to live by them every day. Selected wisely and used diligently to guide your day-to-day actions, your values can be a vehicle that will fast-track you to wherever you want to go. The values you need to improve your life dramatically are rarely the values that come to mind at first when you think of your values.

One of the most important things to consider when choosing your values is what kind of impact you want to have on other people in your life. Often, we think about the impact other people have on us without considering how we impact them. In order to start achieving business and life goals at a level most people only ever dream about, one of your top priorities is thinking about how you react to, and impact, the people you are around.

A second key factor to consider is what kind of values you imagine "future you" would have. Would future you be generous? Would future you be an impressive problem solver? Would future you be bigger than any setback or challenge life could throw your way? Would future you have more authentic relationships? This is important to consider because the sooner you start using your future values to guide your day-to-day behaviors now, the sooner you will become the version of you that you want to be.

A Secret for Speeding up Success

One of the secrets to fast-tracking success is conducting yourself today as though you've already achieved what you want in your future. Most people get this backward; they believe once they have achieved what they set out to do, they will suddenly morph into the person they dream of becoming. Until then, they will continue behaving as they always have. It doesn't work that way.

When you behave like your *next* version of you *now*, your CTO eventually picks up the pattern and turns it into a hot goal. When it does, you will begin to automatically see, say, and do things that will fast-track you to the version of you that you want to be. This is because everything you have, you get more of, and how you behave leads to what you have.

A phenomenon in your brain, coined by neuroscientists as "fire together, wire together," helps us to understand why we always get more of what we have—good and bad. What happens every time you do anything at all is that your neurons fire in a distinct sequence. The more times you do a given thing (like brushing your teeth or doing your grocery shopping), the faster your neurons fire and the more routine the behavior starts to feel. Repeat an action enough times, it becomes a hot goal, also known as a habit or patterned behavior, much like a pony programmed to follow his delivery route.

When it comes to your brain, reinforcement of your patterned behavior becomes stronger and stronger over time (until you do work like you are doing in this book to disrupt patterns that do not serve you). There is an apt quote from the communications trainer and author of *Fierce Conversations*, Susan Scott, which describes the outcome of this phenomenon well: "We succeed or fail, gradually then suddenly, one conversation at a time." Change the word *conversation* to *action* to understand what's going on.

Choosing New Value-Driven Actions

To pick values that will lead to daily behaviors that will lead to the future you want, consider you have achieved everything you wrote about in your three-year, pathfinder vision. Then imagine how you will behave when all those goals have come to fruition, and then adopt those behaviors as values now.

If it helps you imagine how you will behave once you've achieved your goals, look around for people who have achieved what you want and check out their social media pages to get an idea of what some of their core principles might be. You can also read books and watch talks by people who inspire you to learn about their mindset and back-stories and consider which of their values you could embrace to fast-track your success.

Here is a procedure for picking empowering values:

1. Create a laundry list of values you admire and the values or core principles of people whose success you want to emulate. There is no limit to the number of values you can put on this list.

2. Select three or four values that you believe will be the cornerstones of the person you want to be in the future. I suggest no more than three or four, as it's quite difficult to guide your daily behavior by a set of values, and the more values you choose, the less likely it is that you will use them. Don't select values that are already part of your automatic behavior and working for you. Your values should be stretch goals.

3. Create a definition for each of your values. You don't need to use the dictionary definition. Define each value however you want.

It's your value. What's important is that you have a clear understanding of how you should behave because of this value.

4. Write your values down and put them in places where you will see them every day. One of my former program participants placed his chosen values in a frame by his bedside. I have mine on sticky notes on the wall above my computer screen.

5. Convert your values to hot goals one at a time. Pick one of your new values and guide your daily actions and decisions through the lens of this value until you automatically adhere to it. When you start automatically adhering to a value, you will know you've programmed a hot goal to behave in accordance with that value. That's when you pick a new value to integrate into your routine until it becomes a hot goal. Repeat the process of converting empowering values into hot goals one-by-one, and you will be amazed at how quickly your life transforms.

Pro tip: If your values feel easy to live by from the get-go, you're doing them wrong.

Amor Fati

The best way to overcome both predictable and surprise obstacles is to choose a value to overcome obstacles as a way of life. Friedrich Nietzsche was a philosopher who espoused the Latin expression *amor fati*, which means "love fate." Since I've had many serious setbacks, I decided to embrace *amor fati* as a core value so that I would not only focus on overcoming obstacles, but also go a step further and love the situations that challenged me. To achieve this, I force myself to think of ways anything that upsets me could become the best thing that could have happened to me.

Practicing *amor fati* is how I came to think about my car accident with gratitude. Had I not lost everything, had I not learned what it was like to have almost lost my life, I would not have fixated on building a business and life that was perfect for me and stuck with it even after eight years of falling short. I would not have discovered all I did that ended up as this all-in system that has enabled me to create a location-independent business and show others how to do so as well. I didn't see all these positive outcomes at the time of my accident, but if my value back then was to love fate, I might have come to discover the silver linings of my car accident much sooner.

These days when I encounter obstacles and setbacks, I like to practice my *amor fati* value by asking myself a question I picked up from Harv Eker in his book *Millionaire Mind*: "Will I be bigger than this or smaller than this?" It's so succinct, it almost dares me to show up as my best self. It's my first step in my learning to love the frustrations in my life, and it works like a charm. Since changing circumstances typically comes with a fair share of challenging situations, I encourage you to give a value such as *amor fati* a try.

You Have a Destination, Vehicle, and Fuel

Together, your purpose, vision, and values comprise your Happiness Recipe. Consult your Happiness Recipe as you face any decision from now on, and you will commit to courses of action with greater confidence. I like to think of your vision, purpose, and values like a road trip. Your vision is the destination where you ultimately want to arrive. Your values are like a car you drive to get there, and your purpose is the fuel in your tank. With all three, you are sure to arrive at whatever destination you set for yourself.

In the next chapter, you will choose a leap project. Your leap project is a purpose-aligned project that will help you reach your vision on the shortest possible timeline. Before you progress to choosing your leap project, please take a moment to congratulate yourself for all you've done to this point. It's a small minority of people who learn as much about themselves in their whole lives as you've learned about yourself by completing the activities in this chapter. Way to go!

Phase II:

Clarification of Your Target Destination

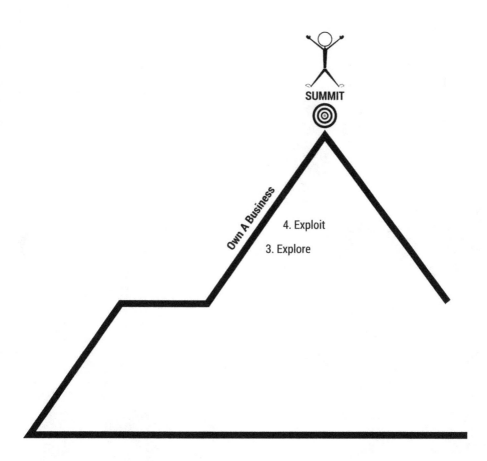

SUMMIT

Own A Business

4. Exploit

3. Explore

CHAPTER 6:

Where to Next?

Back in the nineties, my boyfriend and I were sitting in the back seat of our friend's Toyota Forerunner at the tail-end of a road trip from Toronto to Killington, Vermont. The weather had been bad and the roads snow-covered, which meant the eight-hour drive had taken closer to twelve hours. It was tense inside the car because our driver, Harry, was going rather quickly on winding and slippery mountain roads.

We were all extremely hungry, and it had crossed our minds that if we didn't find the restaurant where we'd made reservations pretty soon, we'd likely not eat in that sleepy town until morning. To complicate matters, we were lost. Sandra, Harry's wife and our navigator, couldn't find the turn we needed to take. Despite driving back and forth on the road where the map indicated the turn should be, we couldn't find it.

Finally, Sandra convinced Harry to pull over so we could hail a passing car for directions. We were lucky enough to stop a local. But our hearts sunk in unison when our savior responded to our request for directions.

In a distinctive Vermont drawl, she immediately told us, "Oh, there? You can't get there from here."

But then, just as quickly as she told us our goal was impossible, she launched into detailed instructions telling us exactly how to get there. Apparently, there was an error on the map, which led many tourists to experience the problem we had. Our stress immediately began to dissipate as we chuckled at the local's paradoxical expression. The lesson for me was that even if it feels like you can't get somewhere from where you are, you probably can. You just need the right map.

I Didn't Have the Right Map

I was forty-eight when I realized I needed to transition from owning a job to owning a business that could make money without me if need be. My car accident had taught me that I couldn't predict when something might suddenly occur that would make it impossible for me to work, and then there were also those circumstances that I could anticipate. Around that time, my father's health declined, and he began to need more care. At the same time, my mother was coming to the end of her ability to live alone in her remote country home that required a great deal of physical labor to maintain. It was clear that I needed more time to help my family. Although my consulting business was doing well, by no means did I have sufficient savings to weather another major work interruption. I wasn't well set up for retirement, either.

I started to think of a business I loved running as a "lifestyle business" because it would enable me to live how I chose. It seemed like an absurdly ambitious idea for someone my age. To say it felt too late was an understatement. The pressure to get my life working in a way that I thought was sustainable caused me to pivot rather abruptly to my new business plan. I stopped seeking entrepreneurial organization clients and started creating online courses and programs for service-based entrepreneurs like myself.

My decision to transition so abruptly led to some lean times. What I didn't comprehend well enough back then is that every time you change what you sell, who you sell to, or how you sell it, you're effectively building a new business. It was one of the most difficult years of my recent career, and there were many times when I wondered if I'd made a decision that would cause me to fall even further behind. After much trial and error, I succeeded in transitioning my business. Looking back, I see how much faster and safer my journey could have been if I'd had a better map.

Let the Band-Aid Fall Off

I encourage a more cautious approach. Even when using the system we teach in Basecamp, it takes our clients about a year to establish a business that has a predictable income. For this reason, I encourage people who are building their business from the ground up to have back-up financial resources for the first year.

For clients seeking to leave their employers, I recommend treating their business as a side hustle until it's clear they will make enough to support themselves. For clients who have already been in business for themselves, I suggest they continue selling what they sold in the past until their new business model has taken root. Whenever you change your niche, positioning, or services, you are effectively building a new business from the ground up, so be prepared to put in the time to get the results you want. Let the Band-Aid of your current income fall off, so to speak, until your new business plan had taken root.

Have you heard of Pareto's 80/20 Principle? It's the idea that twenty percent of the effort you put into something will yield roughly eighty percent of the result. Pareto came up with this idea after noticing that 20 percent of the pea pods in his garden were responsible for 80 percent of the yield. The exact percentages are not the enduring main point. Rather, it's that inputs and results are rarely balanced. You don't need all your time to build a business you love running. You only need to adjust how you spend 20 percent of your time to make incredible things happen for yourself.

I know how hard it is for anyone to find the time—even just 20 percent of our time—to do the kind of work today that makes tomorrow exponentially better. Time and again, I've seen well-intentioned solo entrepreneurs get so wrapped up managing the day-to-day that they struggle to see their way through to carving out time for the kind of work that will pay dividends for the rest of their lives. They feel they will have time for that later. But later never seems to come.

Even the Best-Laid Routes …

Many people who plan to carve out one day a week don't end up following through. I get it. It's tough to build a side hustle when you're already running a business that consumes all of your time. But when I have clients and program participants get real about their aspirations for their futures and about what they can realistically predict their lives will be like, if they don't make substantive changes to their current way of making their living, they realize it's time to lock down that day per week.

One trick to get a full day to yourself each week is to block off two and refuse to sell or give that time to anyone—not to clients, not to family, not to anyone. Why block off two days to get one? Let me explain.

The multiyear consulting gig I took after recovering from my car accident involved the construction and development of the building, management system, and operating procedures for a high-profile restaurant in downtown Toronto called Gusto 101. Over the years, no matter how stressful things got, I was known for maintaining a positive, pragmatic, and solution-finding disposition. (My car accident put the daily stresses of modern work and life into perspective.)

Just before Gusto's opening, I got seriously cranky. It was uncharacteristic of me, and even though there was more work to be done than there were people to do it, my client, Janet Zuccarini, insisted I take three days off. Three full days. It felt like an insane directive. How could I possibly? She calmly explained, "You need one day to rest. Then you're going to need a day to get caught up on your life and your errands. Then you're going to need a day to do something fun. When you've done those three things, you can come back to work."

Janet is a wise business operator. She understands people. Take her lesson to your life. If you're serious about a business that can support you, then you're going to have to find the time to build yourself one. You can approach it the same way you'd build your dream home. You'd live in the place you've got until your new dream home was ready for you to live in full time.

When you carve out two days every week or one full day and two (or three) half days, one is for you to catch up on anything that's behind so you can clear your mind to do your best work. The second is to get that new business working the way you want. If you don't need to catch up on anything, then lucky you. You'll have more time to work on your business, and you'll build—and be able to "move into"—your ideal business even faster.

How to Build an Expertise-Based Business

As I observed earlier, a widespread gap of knowledge about how to efficiently build a business that sells talent and time keeps solo entrepreneurs from achieving their potential. There is so much noise about what to do that it's confusing for anyone without an MBA or similar education to figure out what should be first, second, third, and so on.

Well-meaning practitioners and coaches will tell you that you need brand strategy, content marketing, social media, an online course, a funnel, public relations, systemization, advertising, graphic design . . . the list goes on. In a way, they are right; you may well need all these solutions at various stages in your growth. But there is an order of operations that will make each project more successful as it builds on the last.

When you do the right work at the wrong time, you risk not getting the benefit you hoped. You'll end up spending time and money on things you didn't need, and eventually, you'll find yourself needing to circle back and do it again when the time is right for you.

When it comes to being immeasurably better with your time, one of the smartest things you can do is pick the right project at the right time. In this chapter, we'll take a closer look at the Expertise Business Growth Model (EBGM) and consider some common scenarios to help you think about your current options and figure out what project you want to take on first.

Establishing Your Location on the EBGM

Businesses do one of two things: they solve a problem, or they fulfill a desire. You have developed a skill that you enjoy and sell it to fulfill a need or desire, but your business is inconsistent. It demands too many hours from you, or you cannot step away from it and keep money coming in. If this is the case, then congratulations; on the EBGM, you've made it to basecamp.

The great thing about being at basecamp is that it means you are ready to leverage everything you have learned about yourself, your industry, and your clients, and turn it into your ideal business.

Getting out of Basecamp

Progressing beyond basecamp is a two-phase process. First and foremost, you will want to develop a differentiated signature program or process that you can grow or scale. Growing and scaling are two ways to create a business that could run without you if need be. Growing a business requires you to create a proprietary way of doing things that you can train or certify other people to execute for you. Scaling a business requires you to design your business in such a way that you can increase your revenues without adding a ton of extra labor, cost, or operating expenses.

For example, a website designer might create a proprietary way to build automated sales funnels that help his clients make predictably higher conversions. To grow this business, the website designer can hire or subcontract elements of the work to other people so he isn't limited by his own time or how many clients he can accept.

My client Elaine from the previous chapter is a good example of designing a business model you can scale. Elaine created a membership through which she offers live, weekly group sessions online for all members who attend. There's no limit to the number of people who can attend these sessions, and the sessions require the same time and energy from her regardless of attendance. This is a scalable model.

Like most things, it does not have to be one or the other. My business is a combination of solutions that I can grow or scale. I started online by developing online courses for Skillshare. Whether I get one student or one thousand students per day has no bearing on the amount of work I have to do. Those courses are now products I can scale because they are proven and have outstanding student reviews. To scale them, I would need to develop a profitable advertising campaign that predictably drove traffic to them. Additionally, I can license those same courses to other closed platforms (including my own), enabling me to scale my earning potential from those products even further.

On the other hand, the business programs we offer at BOOM-U are mostly ones we can grow. Although online education can be scalable when delivered as recorded material as in the Skillshare example above, at BOOM-U, we have found that we achieve phenomenal completion and success rates by providing personalized attention and smaller group coaching sessions. Because of our personalized design, as demand for our programs grows, we must hire and train coaches to maintain our standards.

From Basecamp to the Summit

Phase 1: Explore to Start Your Business
The goal of the exploration phase is to prove the viability of your business idea. It is the startup phase where you take ideas and test them to see if they have merit before dumping all sorts of cash or time into them only to find out they're not going to work. Projects to focus on during the exploration phase include:
1. Identify a niche/target market who will buy from you
2. Develop a signature program that satisfies your target market's needs
3. Create back-end offerings for consumers of your signature program
4. Establish your messaging, positioning, and sales conversions

The things you are looking to prove in the exploration phase are that you have a target market that you can reach and who will buy from you, that you have a differentiated signature program, service, or experience at a price that is profitable for you to sell, and that you have marketing or advertising channels that lead to a predictable volume of traffic and eventual sales conversions.

Be a Scrappy Explorer

A scrappy mindset leads to success during the exploration phase. Scrappy, in this case, means that you are spending as little money and time as possible to test each of these steps. Minimum Viable Product (MVP) is a term that's used in tech companies to demonstrate the viability of a solution before major investments are thrown at it. It's essentially the opposite of what a perfectionist would want to create.

For example, if you were testing an idea for a signature coaching or training program, a perfectionist might start by looking around at platforms, creating videos, setting up expensive email servers, and over investing their time on social media. They would spend an inordinate amount of time on behind-the-scenes and busy-work activities like these despite having no evidence that anyone would buy their new idea. Perfectionism is not how to succeed during exploration.

Start with a Beta or Case Study

A scrappy explorer takes an entirely different approach. Starting with about two hours on your hands, you would email and text everyone you knew who might need the kind of results you can make happen with your favorite skill(s) and ask them: "What is the number one problem you badly want solved or desire you wanted fulfilled?" (More often than not, it's easier to get people to pay for a problem they want solved.)

Once you get enough answers back, you are sure to see a need or desire you could serve. That's when you get back to them and say, "Hey, I'm just putting together a program that solves the [need or desire] you told me you have and would get you the results you have been wanting. It's a great opportunity because since I'm building this for the first time, I'm making it a great deal." If they are interested, you don't send them to an impersonal sales page online; you invite them to a phone call, and you have a genuine conversation about the results they need and whether or not you believe you can get them those results.

Even as you accept your first clients, you don't have to worry about exactly how you will get them the results you promised. You have the skillset. You just need the mindset that you will do what it takes to make your beta testing clients over-the-moon happy with the results they get.

The great part about building a signature program by starting with a beta or case study is that your clients know they're getting a deal because they're in on the ground floor. They also know it's not a big risk because you've been in this area for a while and are just repackaging what you know how to do. Even better because you've been upfront about what you're up to, they will be happy to give you their feedback every step of the way, provided you ask for it.

Develop Back-End Services

Have you heard the expression that when one door closes another one opens? Well, that's the way to approach the end of your beta or case study. When you are done and have impressed your clients by over-delivering on their needs, it's time to create a back-end program or services that will serve your clients' needs, ones uncovered by working with you.

For example, people who take Basecamp: Increase Your Impact with a Signature Program want help figuring out a business model that will give them predictable revenue. A Basecamp graduate has a new set of needs: Many want help setting up their marketing, social media, sales processes, tech, and so forth. So, we offer services that meet their new needs. Offering relevant services to the graduates of your initial service or program is critical to your success. It is believed to take fourteen to twenty hours to get a new client using free methods. The sales process for a repeat client is usually one or two hours. Long term, you will run yourself ragged if you try to succeed with a single service or program.

Set up thoughtfully, offering relevant continued support to people who take your program can be a substantial win-win arrangement. In our case, our clients would not only invest far more time and money hiring freelancers to help them, they'd also have to hire and onboard multiple different people or companies, and most of the people they'd hire wouldn't understand their business models.

Many of our clients are initially stressed at the idea of creating a back-end offer because they can't imagine what they'd do. The services we offer at BOOM-U are the exception to the rule. Most back-end programs involve some combination of group coaching, one-to-one coaching, a private community on social media, and some form of accountability. Figuring out a back-end program is easier than most people realize. When you are about three-quarters through your first program, you tell your clients you're considering creating another program for those who want to continue and ask them what help they might want. If you've been all-in on serving them, they will tell you exactly what they want next, and then you build it.

Give Yourself Enough Time

Once you have offered your front-end and back-end experiences three or four times—integrating your client feedback on each iteration—you're almost certainly going to have established a business you can grow or scale. I call this building your business with, rather than for, your clients.

As with your program development, you want to keep your marketing and advertising during exploration scrappy in the beginning. Don't invest hundreds of hours on social media, blogging, content marketing, or advertising. Test various approaches and messaging and see which one predictably leads to buyers for you.

What might surprise you is how long developing a signature program, back-end services, and testing market messaging takes most people. Occasionally, people come to me with next to no mailing list or social media following, expecting millions in sales in their first year. When they do, I tell them Basecamp is not for them because I have no idea how to get a business to those sales quickly. To develop an incredible signature program, back-end services, and testing market messaging takes most of our clients about a year. They can easily make a healthy six figures in that year, depending on their market and price, but $1 million just isn't realistic.

Whether it takes you one year or two years, what's exciting about this business growth model is what comes next. Invest the time to create phenomenal and differentiated programs, get glowing testimonials, and discover the messaging that will predictably lead clients to you. If you do, you'll be so much further ahead than the people who thought the first step was posting daily on social media, starting a podcast, or trying to become an influencer.

It's the rare person indeed who has a proven differentiated program with testimonials. When you put in the effort to create something of actual value, you'll be further ahead than the people who thought they could skip this critical phase of business development.

You are better off going through the exploration phase five or ten times than jumping to the exploitation phase before you're truly ready. Once you have successfully explored an opportunity, you can move to exploiting it quickly.

Phase II: Exploit to Grow or Scale Your Business

Once you've locked down a signature program and back-end offer(s) that are positioned to an exact niche and that your clients rave about, you've proven your business model so you will be positioned to grow or scale. When your business model is proven, it's time to advance to the exploitation phase. The activities to focus on during the exploitation phase have to do with systemization, advertising and publicity, and expansion.

The first step is to secure the time you'll need to grow or scale by removing yourself from the delivery of your services as much as possible. For most of my clients, this means having recordings of their core teachings locked in and hiring former students as coaches. You'll also need a back-office team to help you with the types of activities associated with growth.

Before you take on too many people, it's a good idea to systemize your operations with standard operating procedures (SOPs) for your current model. It makes sense that you will be positioned to create standards once what you sell is standardized. Not only will your team be empowered to do their best when you document your processes, standardizing processes is critical to becoming the owner of a system that can make money with or without you.

The exploitation phase is where you will pick up a megaphone and tell everyone about your signature program, the problem you solve, and for whom you solve it. You do this through activities, things such as strategic marketing, podcast, advertising, public relations, and writing books (such as this one); however, before you jump to focusing on outreach, you'll want to revisit your long-term vision, values, mission, and strategy.

Revisiting your vision, values, mission, and strategy before you jump into growth mode allows you to formally integrate your learnings from your exploration phase. When you take the time to plan this way, you will probably discover there is far more opportunity in your niche then you initially realized. You'll conceive of ways to serve your target market that you can't imagine right now. You might even think of ways to disrupt your industry.

Crystalizing your ideas of the company you want to build is a critical step in improving your leadership. You will most certainly be taking on full-time team members and likely hiring freelancers, too. The bigger you get, the more challenging it is to communicate. The more important it will be that your company directives are out of your head, clearly articulated, and transferred into the hearts and minds of those you enlist to join your journey.

Beware of This Common Mistake

You may need to dip your toe into marketing and advertising during your exploration phase to test your sales process. Other than that, it's not wise to invest heavily in marketing or advertising until you've committed to a niche you want to serve. Considerable resources of time and money are needed to reach a given niche audience. Until you are confident in your audience and what problem you want to solve for them, limit your social media.

Not only will marketing to the wrong audience drain precious time and money, but you'll risk confusing your audience and making a name for yourself even harder. Extensive marketing before you lock in on what you want to become known for goes back to Rory Sutherland's point about people not focusing on hiring the best, but rather on the solution that feels least risky. Until you're confident with what you want to do and for whom, considerable marketing, advertising, and public relations can confuse your market and make doing business with your competition feel less risky than hiring you—not a good idea.

The most efficient way to build an expertise-based business is to find a market you enjoy serving and that will buy from you before creating solutions that address their pressing pain points. Most people do this backward. They think up solutions based on the skills they have and think of all the people who might need them.

The problem with a solutions-first approach is that one of the greatest challenges in business is finding a target market that is willing to buy from you. A far easier endeavor, though it might not seem so until you try it, is creating solutions for a given target market—as I advised you to do to launch your beta or case study and back-end services. The reason it is easier to create solutions for a given market is that all you have to do when you want to create one is ask your clients what they need most. Former clients will tell you what they want. You already have their contact information. You have already built trust.

It's a "you can't get there from here" situation. You can build a thriving profitable business and get to your ideal lifestyle, but the way will be through committing to a niche, creating a signature program your clients rave about, and only then focusing on activities that drive traffic to your sales process.

Don't Fall Victim to the Siren's Trap

Unfortunately, despite the advice about committing to a niche being shared broadly by business experts, many struggling business owners find it challenging to figure out their niche, so they don't do it. Instead, they persist in selling their solutions to multiple target markets (often because they are stressed about money). In doing so, they keep themselves from reaching the financial stability they crave. Like doomed sailors who cannot resist being drawn to the siren's call, so, too, are many aspiring expertise-based business owners struggling who might otherwise have thrived.

I recently gave a presentation at the Centre for Social Innovation, a social-entrepreneurship space in Toronto. I talked about the folly of trying to serve multiple markets. A woman who appeared to be in her fifties approached me afterward and said that—while she understood my points—she believed she could succeed by having multiple niches. It was evident from talking to her that her business was not thriving. I did my best to convince her that a faster way to succeed is to focus on one market and one solution. I fear I failed. As we parted, she told me she was going to stay on her path. She was trapped by the allure of the siren's song.

There is a way to sell to more than one market if you're unrelenting on doing that. But to be successful, you need to realize that each time you identify a new market, you're starting a new business from the ground up (stage one of the explore phase). When you're just adding a new product, you're starting at stage two, which is a step ahead. If you feel you must sell to multiple markets, please be sure to be well into the growth or scaling phase for your first market before starting the exploration phase for the next.

Exploring Your Options

The time has come for you to consider your options for a project you want to focus on as you learn and practice the performance equation. To assist you in your consideration, I describe three scenarios that many of my clients have found themselves in and offer ideas about how to proceed if you find yourself in each scenario. I will refer to the project that you choose at the end of this chapter as your "leap project" because, chosen well, it will accelerate your transition from where you are to where you want to be.

Scenario 1: You've Found What You Love Doing, but Sales are Low

Situation: You've found what you love doing. You're highly credible at doing it. It feels like your calling. Your vision, purpose, and values are aligned, and you know exactly who your market is, but it doesn't seem to be successful enough to continue with it.

This happened to me with the first course I put online. It was called *Maverick's Manifesto*. I'd found a market I was passionate about serving and developed a course my students loved, but my first year offering it online yielded disappointing results. Each time I launched my course, I hoped for twenty to thirty participants but ended up with six to twelve.

Even though my enrollment in *Mavericks* was respectable at the prices I charged, I'd be disappointed because as I learned about putting courses online, I heard about experts in my space who were enrolling a thousand participants and having million-dollar launches. I admit, back then I was one of those people thinking I could just put a course online and make a million dollars.

You know my value of finding a way to love fate? My *amor fati* value? Today, I have come to see that my initial "low" enrollment in *Mavericks* was the best possible thing that could have happened to me (and my program participants).

Acting in accordance with *amor fati*, I decided to follow real estate mogul and *Shark Tank* investor Barbara Corcoran's clever advice from her book, *If You Don't Have Big Breasts, Put Ribbons on Your Pigtails*. Corcoran's advice is captured in her title: Don't try to compete with assets you don't have. Instead, focus on what makes you special. Take anything you currently perceive as a disadvantage and figure out how it can become your advantage.

It's fantastic advice on multiple levels. On a personal level, it helps you celebrate and embrace who you are, as you are, and terminate any goals of wanting to be more like someone else, maybe someone you perceive as more successful than you. On a business level, it helps you create a competitive advantage that is unique to you, and you become the proprietor of a solution that is hard to match.

I Found My Ribbons

Following Barbara's advice, I decided to upgrade my Maverick's course from an impersonal series of recordings and weekly Q&A calls into a high-touch signature program with much more involvement. I started with my key point of difference, my small group sizes, and thought of several ways to turn that into benefits for my clients. I then retooled my curriculum and reinvented the course as a one-of-a-kind personalized and cohort-based experience that people selling evergreen courses with mass enrollments can't compare to.

Because my updated program was much more involved, I changed the name to Basecamp to symbolize that I wanted to work with people who needed to figure out their business model. I also changed the enrollment process. Instead of having a sales page, which allowed anyone with a credit card to sign up, I introduced free discovery calls to ensure we admit only those positioned to succeed.

Without my *amor fati* value or Corcoran's advice to guide me, I might have decided my early trials were proof that things weren't working rather than proof that they were.

How to Select a Leap Project in Scenario 1

You have all your ducks in a row—a clear vision, a specific niche, and a course or offering you have already had some success with—but you are not making the money you need or getting the recognition you hoped. Looking around, you see other people in your field who appear more successful than you. Your desire for more sales is causing your self-confidence to waver. I invite you to consider that you are doing better than you realize. There is a good chance the people who are ahead of you have dared to focus on a single audience and stay in a single game longer.

If you did what I did, put a course online and expected to become a huge sensation out of the gate, consider revisiting that course and turning it into a signature experience like I did when I turned *Mavericks* into *Basecamp*. If you've got something good started but sales are disappointing, resist the urge many people have to quit too early. Look at your situation from more angles. Can what you perceive to be failings become attributes?

When you've found what you love doing, your vision, purpose, and values are aligned, and you adore your market, but your current offering doesn't seem to be successful enough to continue with, consider that maybe all that's needed to bring things about is a few more trials in the exploration phase of your business.

Scenario 2: You've Found What You Love Doing but Not Your Perfect Clientele

Situation: You found what you love, but you don't love the clients you're doing it for. This was my situation after my car accident. I loved helping leaders break through to new levels of performance, but when I was working in entrepreneurial organizations, I didn't enjoy all of the people I had to work with.

My work would start with the CEO. That was usually fun. CEOs of entrepreneurial organizations are brass tacks people who make stuff happen. I like brass tacks people. But after the CEO and I were finished with our groundwork, we needed to bring in members of the team. Some team members were an absolute dream to work with, but others were stuck in their old ways of doing things. I found working with team members who were stuck in the past draining.

Another thing I found draining was the long drive in rush hour to get to and from their offices. After nearly losing my life in my car accident, I loathe driving on highways surrounded by cars whose drivers are in bad moods. Excessive highway time is not living my ideal life.

How to Select a Leap Project in Scenario Number 2

Could I have gotten my consulting business to the exploitation phase and then started the business I'm running now? Absolutely. I could have created and licensed recorded video trainings to help my entrepreneurial clients onboard their new managers. I could have grown by training other consultants and coaches to take on the elements of work I liked least.

Why didn't I? Because this business wasn't aligned with my vision. At the time (which was before I had discovered my purpose of helping dreams come true), I felt called to share my knowledge with as broad an audience as possible. My work in entrepreneurial organizations was helping very successful people become even more so. I saw a world full of people with great ideas and failure rates that were much higher than necessary. I felt called to share this information with people like me, who I believed needed it more.

If you've got something that's working, but it's not aligned with your vision, then you must make the decision only you can make. What is your best way forward? You might decide to walk away, like I did. You might decide you're so close to the exploitation phase that you stick with your current way of making money until you build your business to the point where you can hand off operations or sell it. You might decide something else. But you would do well to decide whether you're willing to stick with a business that doesn't feel like it's your calling and for how long.

Scenario 3: You Need Money – Your Perfect Business Can Wait

Situation: You need money. Your income has dried up, and you don't have sufficient savings to buy yourself some time. Your top priority is making money and paying your bills.

Sometimes people tell themselves they're cash strapped when they're not. They stress about money because they lost a client or a job, even though they have ample savings to tide them over for a period of time. Then there are those times where you just need money. I've been in both situations more than once and so have my clients and program participants.

If I was in the first situation, I would prioritize picking a leap project that I could turn into my ideal business. If I were in the second situation, genuinely about to lose my home or have the power shut off, then I would prioritize stabilizing my cash flow until I felt safe enough to take those two days off a week to start building my ideal business.

When Your Need for Money is Urgent

My brother, Owen Steinberg, was in the second situation around the time the COVID-19 situation hit. Owen is a top-caliber chef. I know this sounds like sisterly love talking, but it's not just me who thinks so. He's won awards. Dozens of articles have been written about his culinary abilities over the years, and he has wowed diners that hail from some of the best food cities worldwide. He is also interested in protecting our food systems with sustainable farming practices and was a farm-to-table chef long before that was a thing.

Five years before the COVID-19 shutdowns, Owen opened a casual food restaurant that offered consciously-sourced foods available at everyday prices—some of the produce was grown on a small farm he ran. Due to large initial capital investment and a slow start getting the word out in the first year, the business accumulated substantial debt before turning a profit. For the next four years, the profits fed the debt.

When business ground to a halt, the resources were not there to pay the bills and accumulated debt, so my brother decided to close the restaurant. When this happened, his income evaporated while his life expenses carried on. With a young son to care for, a home to maintain, and his savings lost to the restaurant's debts, Owen's top priority became replacing his restaurant's income. Building a dream business was far from his mind.

Over several dinners, we talked about hot goals. I was concerned about hot goals regarding loss that might have been established when we were growing up. When we were in our teens, our father, who was mentally ill, borrowed heavily against our family home. When mortgage rates spiked, my father lost our home to the bank. These are the kinds of past events that can lead to hot goals.

Owen agreed that his top priority was exploring his unwanted hot goals and laying down new ones aligned with prosperity. Using the activities included in this book, he identified limiting hot goals and started reprogramming new ones. His spirits rose in a matter of weeks; he knew what he wanted to do next. He decided to make himself available as a private chef. He updated his website, offering private dinner events and catering. All he needed to get the word out was to send emails and texts and let his fans over the years know what was going on.

Bookings started coming in, which took care of his immediate financial needs. Turning his attention to creating a signature experience, Owen identified his target market as home cooks who are bored in the kitchen and want to make healthy and delicious meals their family will love. Then he created his program, The Quizzical Chef.

Ever wonder why something as basic as chicken tastes so much better from your favorite restaurant? It's not the recipe; it's the technique. Chefs are trained on how to work with food regardless of the recipe, so no matter what ingredient you have on hand, you know how to bring out its best. So he teaches his students to cook the way professional chefs do — with a focus on technique.

The lesson I want you to take away is, Owen got money coming in first and designed his signature program second. Businesses based on signature programs take a year or more to establish, so if you are in a state of financial urgency, take care of your immediate income needs first.

How to Select a Leap Project in Scenario Number Three

Remember: Always start where you are. If you're fretting about money but have an income coming in and savings in the bank—just not as much as you would like—then perhaps consider how you might modify your expenses for a period of time so you can take those one or two days a week and build a signature program, which you can grow or scale.

If, however, like my brother Owen after his restaurant closed or me in debt after my car accident, you need to get cash flow going for stability, then the wisest course of action is likely a return to the industry and skillset in which you're already established. Once you're financially stable again, you can see what more might be calling you.

Whether you are fretting about money while sitting on substantial savings or are truly without the income you need, your number one most critical course of action in scenario number three is figuring out what cycle from your past you are repeating and programming new and more prosperous hot goals.

Did I end up in that car accident as a way to ensure I'd lose everything? I can never know. I do know that my consulting career was on the rise back then, and I had hot goals from my childhood about loss. In addition to losing our family home, my parents also lost their once-thriving remedial-education school. Whatever your CTO is programmed to accomplish, it will find a way to bring about. The lesson to remember is whenever you want something different than what you have, replacing old hot goals is always the place to start.

It's Decision Time

In this chapter, you've considered what your leap project will be. We took a closer look at creating a signature program or experience to build an expertise-based business you can grow or scale. We reviewed the activities to focus on during the exploration and exploitation phases and learned why a scrappy mindset gets you farther than a perfectionist one. We examined three scenarios that many people who sell their time and talent find themselves in and what kind of leap project might be right for you at this time.

If you're ready to build a signature program you can eventually grow or scale, my advice is to remember that the process takes my clients the better part of a year to follow all the steps. Although you will make money during the first year, you may prefer to maintain stability in by following Pareto's Principle and committing two days per week for your exploration so you can ensure you get at least one. I advise against jumping in as I did, but rather treat it like a side hustle and switch to your new business model only when you've done enough exploration to be confident it will work.

The project you choose now—your leap project—will be the focus for the rest of this book as we switch our attention focus to the performance equation component of your all-in system. In the next chapter, we'll get started with the first step of the performance equation, setting a goal statement for your leap project, and taking steps to ensure you translate your goal statement into a language your CTO can understand.

Introducing Goal-ology

A final note before we switch to the performance equation. One thing that gets tricky in the goal biz is terminology. For example, you have a purpose, which is a biological hot goal; a vision, which is a compelling meaningful goal for your future; projects, that work within a specific time frame to achieve your vision and purpose; and the list goes on. There are goals within projects, subgoals within goals, sub-subgoals within subgoals. Then, of course, there are your conscious goals and your CTO's hot goals. Within hot goals are those you do want, those you don't want, and those you are trying to program.

You can see how all this goal talk can get confusing pretty quickly. To align our terminology, I created a short appendix on "Goal-ology," which you can find at the end of this book. I encourage you to have a peek at it before continuing on to the next chapter.

CHAPTER 7:

Who Needs Willpower?

his is the point in your all-in system that we move from getting on the best possible route to showing you how you can progress farther faster with Ferrari-level performance tools. You are going to be amazed at how much more you bring about for yourself when you apply the performance equation.

Once you have identified a leap project that is aligned with your purpose and moving you closer to your vision, it's time to craft a compelling goal statement that captures what success looks like, which simultaneously gets your CTO on board with your plans. To achieve this, I will teach you a goal statement development tool I call the MOMA Method.

MOMA stands for Motivating Outcomes with Measurements that are Aligned with your Happiness Recipe. The method enables you to accomplish two significant objectives at the beginning of any project. First, it helps you raise your expectations of what success will look like. Second, it translates your goals from the language of your conscious brain, concept, and ideas, into the language your CTO understands, senses, and feels.

When you start every project or initiative by developing a goal statement using the MOMA Method, you will speed up the process of establishing your conscious goals as hot goals. While you can certainly drum up willpower and force yourself to work on a project that is not backed up by a hot goal, relying on willpower for any length of time will lead to you underperforming. You will go farther faster when your CTO is conditioned to automatically take action in the direction of what you want.

Before I walk you through how to use the MOMA Method, I will illustrate why traditional goal-setting methods fall into the Fiat category of achievement.

(Not So) SMART Goals

Despite many success and leadership coaches having debunked SMART goals, the method is still broadly used. There are several definitions of SMART goals. The following comes from Gary Latham and Edwin Locke's goal gospel, *New Developments in Goal Setting and Task Performance*. SMART stands for specific, measurable, attainable, results-oriented, and timely. While SMART goals work well enough for creating subgoals, but they're woefully lacking when it comes to creating goal statements for significant projects.

As I explain in the Goal-ology appendix, the term "goal" is one few people use accurately. Merriam-Webster online defines a goal as "the end toward which effort is directed." Clear enough, except how it is more often used is to describe what you think you must do to get to another outcome. An easy example here is to think of anyone with the goal of going to the gym. Most likely, being at a gym would not be someone's endpoint. There is a much better chance that someone with the goal of going to the gym is seeking an endpoint of being fit and healthy, and going to the gym is actually a strategy step, something they feel they must do to obtain that result.

Not an Endpoint

Nowhere in SMART goals are you required to pay attention to whether or not you're focusing on an actual endpoint, which is the entire point of creating a goal statement. Results-oriented comes close but still just points toward the end rather than taking you to the end itself.

Take Melissa's goal. Melissa was a client of mine who streamlined her branding services business by creating a signature program. Melissa wanted to build a business she didn't need to work in every day. A signature program was an excellent choice for a leap project since she already had a proven niche market she enjoyed. When she first shared her goal statement with me, she wrote, "Create a signature program."

At first glance, this might seem like a reasonable goal statement, and if you were using the SMART method, it might meet all the criteria but the M (measurable). But Melissa's goal statement did not accurately convey the real outcome she sought. After using the MOMA Method, we ended up with "I have an in-demand signature program that my clients find valuable, that I am proud of and enjoy providing, and that I would not need to be involved in if I decided to step away from the business."

As you can see, Melissa's second goal was way more exciting than her first one, which, in retrospect, was rather boring. Her target outcome and what it meant to her life were evident in reading the goal she developed with the MOMA Method. This is why my top issue with the SMART goal-setting method is that it does not have a letter that reminds you to describe your endpoint.

Crummy Plans

SMART goals lead us to drab goals. On top of that, by not focusing on our endpoints, we end up with limiting plans. Take a moment and discover this for yourself. Grab a notebook and do a quick back-of-the-napkin brainstorm for Melissa's before and after goal statements. (Note: You'll learn more if you stop now and do this quick activity.)

What happened? For her original goal, "create a signature program," you might come up with a bunch of ideas that could be executed in a month or two. Brainstorm ideas for her topic, create training outlines, produce videos and worksheets, pick a platform to host her program on, pick some days/times to do group coaching or one-to-one coaching, decide how much she wants to charge, and voilà, her plan might be considered done.

The plan for Melissa's MOMA-fied goal statement would need to be more robust. It would almost certainly involve building her program in active collaboration with clients to ensure her clients find it "invaluable." She'd need to figure out compelling market positioning, so her program becomes "in-demand." She would need to create a process to regularly check in with herself to ensure she was enjoying work. And she'd need to plan for how she could systemize and train others so she could eventually "step away from her business."

If you want greater project successes, then you want to make sure the goal statements you develop for your projects move you in that direction. In Melissa's case, we weren't just interested in a signature program. We needed a signature program her clients would happily pay for, which would become "in-demand" and create the foundation for a business that would give her financial stability. When the goal is inferior, so too will your plan be inferior and, subsequently, your results. Not cool, SMART goals.

Not Motivating

Another issue with the SMART tool is the complete lack of motivation in the process. Recently, a number of experts have asserted that our goals don't have to be motivating and that we can just force ourselves to do things. They are correct; you do have the ability to push projects from your conscious brain and get the job done. But just because you can force yourself to do something doesn't mean that's your best option.

As I've mentioned before, you can force yourself to do things from the conscious part of your brain, but it will be exhausting, and there goes your quality of life. It's such a needless waste when it's not that difficult to get your CTO on board. Forcing yourself to do things you're not motivated to do is a solution that may work for people in corporate, who may have accepted they don't need to enjoy their work, but it's a terrible idea when you work for yourself and are committed to enjoying your life.

You want your goals to be intrinsically motivating because that's a way you can speak to your CTO. Your CTO is determining most of what you see, say, and do, and when it's on board with your goals, you will be exponentially more effective with your time.

How do you get your CTO to be on board with your goals? By developing a goal statement in such a way that just thinking about your goal intrinsically feels motivating and triggers positive emotions. When your CTO feels positive emotions, it understands this is something you want and subsequently starts to program hot goals. Repeat the sequence of thinking of a motivating goal and feeling good about it enough times, and soon enough, you will have a fully-developed hot goal and a CTO that is causing you to see, say, and take action on things that move you in the direction of success.

So no, you don't need your goals to motivate you, but you are short-changing yourself by skipping this step. If it's possible to pursue a goal that brings you joy and excitement instead of approaching it as a chore, why wouldn't you? With fifteen to twenty minutes, you can take most goals from mundane to exciting with the MOMA Method, and doing so will increase productivity and add joy to your life. It would be a real shame to leave such a valuable benefit off the table.

Attainable (Yawn)

I'm not a fan of the A (attainable) in SMART because it pretty much eliminates the creation of stretch goals. If Thomas Edison had used the SMART method, would he have invented the lightbulb? Would we have the Internet, cell phones, solar power, or space travel? Entrepreneurs create from nothing; a bit of unreasonableness goes along with that. While I don't encourage my clients to go after endeavors that would put them at risk, I do believe the most exciting businesses and lives are created by consistently taking on goals just beyond our comfort zones.

Very small shifts in trajectory can make big differences in where you end up. Your goal statement is describing your endpoint, not where you are. I encourage you to set goals that are on the edge of your belief that you can accomplish them. It's a practical approach to ending up dramatically more successful. I find the sweet spot of challenge is when you find yourself flip-flopping between being certain you can achieve a goal and wondering if you've set your sights on a target that is a tad too ambitious.

Introducing the MOMA Method

To address the shortfalls of the SMART system, I created the MOMA Method. By developing goal statements that introduce your goals to your intellect and your emotions, you will implant your goals into your conscious mind and subconscious. Although the MOMA Method will be indispensable for your business, I strongly recommend you use it in all facets of your life. If you need to plan a wedding or move homes, or if you want to make a health and fitness change, with the MOMA Method, you'll speed up the critical process of onboarding your CTO.

Right now, it's time to use the MOMA Method for your leap project. Grab a notebook and a pen and get started.

Create a MOMA Goal Statement

Start with MO: What is Your Motivating Outcome?

Figure out a motivating outcome for your leap project (or any project) with this activity:

1. Write down your goal as it comes to mind, without worrying about getting it right.
2. Explore the outcome or endpoint of the goal you wrote down by listing all the reasons you can think of for wanting it. To do this, ask yourself, "Why do I want to achieve this goal?" at least six or seven times. Only stop asking/answering when you run out of answers because the best answers often come after you ask a question

six or seven times. (I call this the SixX method and will ask you to use it throughout the application of the performance equation.)

3. Using the SixX method, get your CTO to tune into its job of protecting you by listing all the possible unwanted consequences you might face if you don't achieve this outcome.

4. Using the SixX method, get your CTO to tune into its job of helping you thrive by listing all the possible positive consequences you might enjoy if you do achieve this outcome.

5. Looking back at the goal you wrote down in step one, rewrite your goal statement until it captures what you want most and thinking about achieving it makes you smile involuntarily.

6. Repeat steps two to five until you figure out an outcome you're super stoked to bring about.

M: How will You Measure Success?

Determine meaningful measures of success with this activity:

1. Imagine yourself on a specific day in your future after having achieved your motivating outcome. Pick a day three years out from the day you are reading this. Imagine you have achieved everything you want in this scenario. From this place of achievement three years from now, look around at what's happening in your life:
   - What is this day in your future like from start to finish?
   - Where are you, and what are you doing?
   - Who are you with, and what are you like?
   - Notice what is and isn't in your life
   - Notice how you feel

2. Select measurements. Considering your answers to the questions above, select meaningful measures of success, objective occurrences that will prove to you and anyone looking over your shoulder that you have achieved your MO (motivating outcome).

3. Choose timelines for each measurement. Some measurements will take longer to achieve than others. For example, if you have an income goal of $300,000 or better per year but you have no income from a signature program now, that would take most clients following my system two years to achieve.

A: Ensure Your Goal is <u>A</u>ligned

Use these questions to ensure your goal is aligned to your Happiness Recipe.

1. How is your goal aligned with your purpose?
2. How will this goal move you in the direction of your vision?
3. How will you be able to express your values by working toward this goal?
4. In what ways is your goal good for others (i.e., your clients, collaborators, family)? (All business goals should be seeking win/win/win outcomes.)
5. How badly do you want this goal? On a scale of one to ten, with one being "meh" and ten being "as much as I've wanted anything," is this goal what you want? If you do not rate this goal as a nine or ten, return to the MOM steps to craft a more motivating outcome and/or measures of success.

Melissa's MO

Let's return to Melissa's MO, "I have an in-demand signature program that my clients find valuable, that I am proud of and enjoy providing, and that I would not need to be involved in if I decided to step away from the business" to understand how you might select measures of success and test your alignment to a goal.

Melissa's Measurements

- I have a signature program I am proud of offering.
- My sales are over $120,000 in the first year, and I double my sales every year after that.

- My positioning is so clear that in year two or three I get invited to speak once per month or more at events, podcasts, or summits.
- By my second year, my program will be so in-demand that I am running a waitlist.
- 80–100 percent of my participants give glowing recommendations and refer others.
- 50–70 percent of my participants capture momentum by signing up for my back-end programs.
- I can easily afford a virtual assistant and hire a team to help me run this program.
- I wake up every day, super excited to be involved in this experience.
- I feel lighter and more grounded.
- I am more present with my family.
- I am working less and making more than I am making now.

Melissa's Alignment

- Melissa's pathfinder vision involved being able to spend quality time with her children and husband, so creating a business that she could step away from was important.
- Melissa's goal was good for her clients because they experienced more predictable results, controlled pricing, and had clear outcomes; it was good for her collaborators because she could create jobs. It was good for her family because she could have more time with them that she would enjoy.
- Melissa's desire was a ten. She had spent years working in an exhausting job in marketing, and she couldn't bear the idea of a life that didn't give her more freedom.

Hey, Where's the Project Deadline?

You may have noticed the conspicuous absence of any deadlines in the MOMA Method. When I teach MOMA as a stand-alone goal development tool, I do have people set something I refer to as appointments for review, but when I teach it as part of my all-in system, timelines are better handled during planning.

Unless a deadline is set in stone or you are guaranteed to meet it, my experience is they can do more harm than good during goal setting. Whenever you are setting a goal for something you have not done several times before (which is almost every goal when you're building a business you can grow or scale), there is almost no chance that you will know in advance all the subgoals, sub-subgoals, and tasks required to accomplish each project. If you don't know what success will require, how can you accurately predict how long you will need?

Meaningless guesses on deadlines can become a risk because of the new relationship you're forming with your CTO. If you set erroneous dates for goals that you don't keep, it can backfire on your morale, particularly if you've been struggling with distraction or procrastination. Part of getting you to believe that you can reach a higher level of success than the one you have now is going to require getting your CTO to witness you getting new things done. If you make a habit of setting deadlines you don't keep, you program your CTO to fall short of your aspirations. This process puts you at risk of feeling bad about yourself and of a heightened emotional state that would reinforce hot goals you don't want.

When I teach my complete performance equation, I have you set deadlines only once you've completed robust planning and have a more realistic sense of the various subprojects your leap project is going to take to achieve. When you have a better sense of what you will need to do to achieve a goal, you will establish more realistic timelines and build a more productive relationship with your CTO.

Onboarding Your CTO

Now that you have your MOMA goal statement for your leap project, your next step is ensuring your CTO is on board. If you are lucky, the project you selected will not be in conflict with any other hot goals you have. If that's the case, the MOMA goal-statement development process might have been enough to get your CTO taking the lead.

In the event you do have conflicting hot goals, you don't just need to program your CTO; you need to *re*program your CTO, and there are additional steps to achieve that.

If you've wanted to build a better business for any length of time and you have not succeeded, it's likely that you have conflicting hot goals limiting your success and will need to take the additional reprogramming steps. At first, it annoyed me that I'd have to go to such lengths to get my CTO to switch hot goals; then, I started to think about it differently.

What Would Your Best Friend Do?

Say you've always wanted to take a trip to Paris. You've dreamt about it all your life. You've told your best friend hundreds of times that you want to go there. Then, suddenly, a client takes a trip to London, tells you about it, and you decide you want to go to London instead. You share your new desire to go to London with your best friend over a drink.

Let's imagine this creates a conundrum for your best friend. Your best friend has been secretly planning to take you on a surprise trip because you have a big birthday coming up. Your best friend has been planning the trip to Paris for months. Now, all of a sudden, you're going on about London. Your bestie doesn't want to ruin the surprise, so where will she decide to take you? All she ever remembers you talking about is Paris. Then out of the blue, you mention London. Since you wanted Paris for a lifetime, that's probably where she's going to end up taking you. It just feels more important since you've mentioned it hundreds of times.

That's how I understand the dichotomy between the goals of your conscious and subconscious brain. Repetition wins. If your current project is somehow in conflict with an established hot goal, your CTO (best friend) is going to need some convincing. You will always know when your CTO is on board with a goal because you will automatically be taking action and making progress on it.

Thinking Vitamins

For important projects, always assume there is a counter goal. The sooner you uncover any hot goals that are holding you back, the sooner your CTO will gladly take over and move you in the direction of your dreams.

When I began teaching online programs, I set my mind on a goal I had little faith in. I'd set the target of reaching ten thousand students online. At the time, the number was pure madness to me. Until then, I had been working for entrepreneurial CEOs and their management teams, which involved working with a few dozen people every year.

The idea of having ten thousand students seemed highly unlikely. I had written the goal on my bathroom mirror, and every time I brushed my teeth, I'd get sweaty palms. It seemed so impossible. Why would anyone want to learn about business and productivity from me when there are already so many established people teaching it in the marketplace?

Two years later, I had over 18,000 students on Skillshare, which is just one of my platforms! I made it happen—this goal, which seemed impossible, was possible. A big part of how I managed to reprogram my CTO was with a tool I call Thinking Vitamins. Thinking Vitamins is a list of questions that speak directly to your CTO. Each time you ask and answer the questions, you take another step toward programming a goal into a hot goal.

I like the idea that they're vitamins because we don't expect a vitamin to make us healthy the moment we pop it in our mouths, but if we take it over time, it can have a cumulative positive effect.

When I first created Thinking Vitamins, I was pretty much in a constant state of negative self-talk. I wasn't good enough, didn't have enough friends, didn't like my home, didn't have enough money. I could go on and on. There was pretty much nothing I didn't need to improve. Thinking Vitamins helped me tackle each of these and more.

I will be sharing the full process for Thinking Vitamins in Chapter 10 (after you've developed your road map), but here is a starter set of vitamins you can start taking now:

Complete these statements in the morning and before settling into work on your project:

- My purpose (acorn) is ...
- My leap project is connected to my purpose (acorn) because ...
- Three or more awesome things that will happen if I achieve my leap project are ...
- This will be good for other people (clients, family, collaborators) in my life because ...
- Three or more reasons I have what it takes to achieve my leap project are ...
- Even if I encounter setbacks, I can achieve my leap project because ...
- Three or more things I am grateful for about my current situation (business and life) are ...
- Actions I've already taken toward my leap project are ...
- I can and will bring joy as I work toward this project because ...

Finish by imagining the future moment when you achieve your leap project and connect to feelings of gratitude for trusting in your success.

Cleaner Teeth

I have my Thinking Vitamins posted in my bathroom. I do this so there's no excuse for me to forget to take them every day or to pretend I don't have time. If you have time to brush your teeth, you have time to reprogram your CTO to lay down hot goals that will lead you to your dreams. You can download a copy of Thinking Vitamins from https://www.jillmcabe. com/itsgotime_rabbit.

Create a Motivating Nickname

Creating a motivating nickname for important projects will help get your CTO on board. Take time to choose one that captures the endpoint and also how you want to feel after you've achieved your project. Here are a few examples: A couple of years ago, when we moved my mom out of her country home (which had three buildings and twenty years of accumulated treasures), we named her goal Smooth Move—and it was. One of my clients who couldn't stand doing financial work and needed to get that part of her business in order named her project Beauty and the Books. Speak Easy was the inspiring name another client came up with for their signature public speaking program. When you create fun nicknames for your goals, you make them intrinsically more motivating, which is part of the language your CTO understands.

I post the nickname for any important project I am actively working on in multiple places where I can see it. For me, the best spots are on a large note just above my computer screen and next to my Thinking Vitamins on my bathroom mirror. In addition to speeding up the programming of my hot goals, it's a great way of reminding me of my active priorities.

Create a Visual

One risk with traditional vision boards is that they can become too cluttered. For every important project or goal, you want to create a stand-alone visual that gets your emotions fired up when you look at it. Choose a photograph that inspires you. Mock up a magazine article with a heading about you, create a business card with a new title and put it in your wallet, or mock up that cover for the book you want to write. One of my program participants who was working on a movie bought a replica Oscar statue. Whatever you choose, make sure it represents success to you and also elicits positive emotions that your CTO will have no choice but to notice.

Make sure to put this visual somewhere you will see it repeatedly each day.

Cheer for Your Competition

I used to feel down when I thought of people I perceived to have similar skills to mine but who were more well-known than me. I was worried their success meant there wasn't room in the market for me to do the things I wanted to do. What I have since learned is there is room for everybody.

There are billions of people on this planet, and just because somebody is making money doing what you want to do doesn't mean there isn't space for you. It means there *is* space for you. It means that people like to buy that thing. You know what people like? They like choices. They like customization. They love finding their tribe.

A critical reason you need to cheer for your competition has to do with hot goals you need to program. Remember, your subconscious is physiologically wired to protect you from anything bad or unsafe. If you look at a person who has a business you envy and thinking about it conjures negative feelings, you are telling your brain that having a business like the one they have is unsafe for you. Your brain cannot differentiate between bad for someone else and good for you. The takeaway: Cheer for your competition whose businesses you admire, and your CTO will set hot goals to help you emulate their results. You'll feel happier, too.

The Payoff for Hot Goals

You have two choices when it comes to accomplishing something. You can force yourself to do it from the conscious part of your brain, which will take a considerable amount of effort and attention—an exhausting proposition that you are unlikely to enjoy.

Or, you can take some extra time up front to establish a hot goal so your CTO is on board. When you take the time to establish hot goals for your important undertakings, you will have two parts of your brain working on your goal simultaneously. Critically, you will have the part of your brain that takes on the lion's share of determining your daily actions working on your goal.

It's inevitable that some of your goals will be in conflict with prior hot goals. When this happens, programming a hot goal may take longer, but it will happen if you follow the steps in this chapter enough times. When it comes to the brain, repetition wins. You simply have to communicate to your CTO that you want to go to London more times than you communicated that you wanted to go to Paris. The older you are, the longer this can take.

There are going to be times where your CTO is going to hide some of your former hot goals from you. I encourage you not to get frustrated when you discover unwanted hot goals. When you get frustrated with your CTO, you're getting mad at a younger, more fragile version of yourself; instead, just say, "Cool, good to know; things went down in the past, and this is where I turn that situation to my advantage." Even if you don't know how long it will take you to turn that situation around, if you hold it in your mind that you will prevail, then you will.

Repetition Reprograms

This is what happened with my brother, Owen. After closing his restaurant, he took a while to regroup. When he first began identifying his unwanted hot goals and reprogramming new ones, not much changed. Then one day, as he describes it, he just started acting on progressive ideas. With his hot goals now updated, making progress became natural.

You and your CTO are at the beginning of what has the potential to be a beautiful relationship. It may take you some time to get blissfully in sync on a given goal, but there's no leaving this CTO. You're together forever so it makes good sense to invest in this relationship. Every moment you are frustrated, you are digging your hole deeper; every moment you spend conditioning yourself with positive thoughts, emotions, and images, you are climbing out.

Taking time to program hot goals for what you want is one of the highest payoff performance activities in which you can invest your time. As you develop your mastery, you will start working toward your goals automatically. This is what I mean by the title of this chapter, "Who Needs Willpower?" When you start each project by creating a goal statement using the MOMA Method and take the extra steps in this chapter to program your CTO, drumming up willpower every step of the way will be a thing of the past.

It's Time to Create an Incredible Plan

Congratulations on reaching the end of Phase II. You figured out your current coordinates; you've clarified your target destination and selected a leap project to work on; you've created a goal statement that lights your fire every time you think about it; and you've started the process of (re) programming your CTO to take over as lead on your project. You've earned the right. It's time to plan.

Phase III:

Plans for an Easier Approach

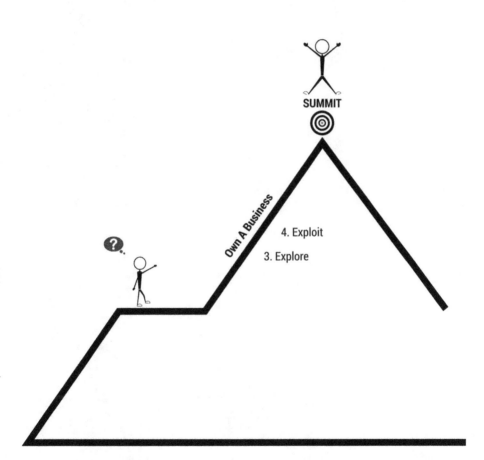

CHAPTER 8:

Better Road Maps

H as this happened to you? You got going on a project you were excited about and then just stopped working on it. You're not sure what happened. You lost your focus and motivation. In many cases, it turns out that coming up short or abandoning projects altogether can be traced to insufficient planning. A common approach to creating plans is to start with a bit of brainstorming, make a few gut decisions, and maybe throw in some quickly-chosen deadlines to make the process feel organized. One of the greatest disservices you can do to yourself is this kind of (Fiat-level) planning.

Whatever your leap project is, it's almost certain to have several, if not dozens, of subprojects. The level of detail you will need for your leap project plan and subproject plans differ. A leap project takes months and sometimes years to achieve, and, much like the back-of-the-napkin plans you created to consider new ways to make more money, they only require enough big-picture thinking to give you and your CTO confidence that you have a plausible case for success. Subprojects are more immediate and have clear, visible finishing lines. Plans for your subprojects benefit from what I refer to as a nitty-gritty level of detail.

To begin this chapter, you will create what I call a staircase strategy: a thoughtfully-considered series of subprojects that, if taken, will get you from the bottom to the top—the top of the staircase representing the successful completion of your leap project. Some of the activities in the chapter may feel familiar. Still, like everything in this book, we will be approaching the development of your staircase strategy using refined techniques, such as how to word your planning questions to elicit better ideas and onboard your CTO in the process.

Once you've identified the subprojects of your staircase strategy, you will sequence these subprojects in the order you believe you might follow to achieve them. Then you will identify which subproject you will work on first. The subproject you identify to tackle first will become your active assignment and the focus of the second half of this chapter. You will develop a nitty-gritty plan for your active assignment.

During the nitty-gritty planning, I will introduce powerful planning techniques informed by psychology and behavioral science research.

Brainy Brainstorming

Psychiatrist Iain McGilchrist, author of *The Master and His Emissary: The Divided Brain and the Making of the Western World*, teaches about the left and right hemispheres of our brains. Your right hemisphere receives new ideas. Your left hemisphere organizes and rearranges ideas but is unable to acquire new ones. We can only engage one hemisphere of our brain at a time, so you're either open to new ideas or rearranging ones you already have but never doing both at the same time.

This is where effective brainstorming techniques become indispensable. To build a business you love running, you will forever have to take on projects in areas in which you have little prior experience. Since you certainly want to capitalize on new and better ideas, brainstorming, when correctly approached, is an activity that can help you achieve this.

Brainstorming is a process everybody seems to be able to explain, but few can do. Most people know they are supposed to have an open mind when they brainstorm, but when I guide uninitiated clients in this activity, I don't often see it. For example, most people would tell you to accept all ideas in brainstorming, but humans seem to have an instinctively hard time doing so. We all know and have heard that wild, crazy, and fun ideas can be the ones that lead you to the idea you need, but somehow when these ideas come up during brainstorming, there's this immediate reaction from our CTOs saying, "No, that's ridiculous; that won't work."

When that happens, you move immediately from the right hemisphere to the left hemisphere of your brain, from an atmosphere that was open to new ideas to one that can only rearrange the ideas it already has. The whole point of brainstorming is to come up with new ideas, so to succeed, you have to remain open.

To achieve this when brainstorming, write down every idea that you come up with—no matter what. If your CTO pipes up, "That's crazy," "That'll never work," "That's too much," "You tried that before and failed," calmly disregard these quips. Such judgments will immediately shut down your right hemisphere. Without new ideas to work with, your left brain will never get its time to shine. If your CTO is squawking at you, be gracious and firm as you tell your CTO that you promise to choose the best ideas later, but you need some fresh ideas first.

Your Staircase Strategy Brainstorm

To initiate a brainstorming session, look at your MOMA statement for your leap project and ask yourself, "How could I do this? How else could I do this?" As with activities earlier in this book, use the SixX questioning method described in Chapter 7 to come up with as many ideas as you can. Once you open the dam, let ideas flow without judgment, and you will be amazed at the creative ideas you come up with. As you consider how you will achieve the various elements of your leap project, remember to look at your original MO statement, as well as each of the success measures you chose. Typically, you can expect each success measure you identified to become its own subproject.

Use Conditional Language

Take a moment to look more closely at the question, "How could I do this?" Did you notice I used the word "could" instead of the word "will" or "should?" The reason you want to use conditional language during idea generation is that it makes answering feel safe. When you ask questions such as "How *will* I achieve this?" you are creating pressure to get the answer correct, which in turn risks you triggering your left hemisphere to take over, and idea generation is the time for your right hemisphere to do its thing.

Your goal during brainstorming is to come up with ideas so clever that you're amazed you thought of them. Only your right hemisphere will enable you to do that. Brainstorming sessions are your safe space to be original, outlandish, and risky. If you swap over to your left hemisphere, the doors shut, and the flood of fresh ideas will dry up. To keep your right hemisphere engaged and the possibilities flowing, always ask brainstorming questions using conditional language.

I encourage you to start asking more questions with conditional language so you can see how it works in action. For the rest of this week, notice how you respond to questions that use conditional language versus questions that use absolute language. If you ask questions of others, notice how they respond to these differences. You are sure to discover how much safer it feels to respond to conditional language.

Look for the Easy Way

I'd be remiss if I didn't point out a simple but powerful time-saving question to ask during brainstorming. If you've been working hard for less than optimal results, you've probably been raised with some version of the tenet that hard work pays off: the idea that if you don't have sweat on your brow at the end of the day, you haven't accomplished anything. The clear risk in believing in hard work is that your CTO will set hot goals for your work to be hard. As long as the idea is reinforced, the harder work will become. Ask anyone with a successful business and they will tell you that making more money is easier than making less.

The truth is there's almost always a simpler way to do things than the one you first considered. People who achieve extraordinary results are the ones who see paths you didn't, shortcuts you missed. The fun part? To get yourself finding new and easier solutions, all you have to do is ask for them. Ask yourself questions such as these:

- What is an easier way I could do this?
- What is an even simpler way I could achieve this?
- If there was an even easier way, what would it be?
- Who would know an easier way to achieve this?

You get the idea. Just keep playing with questions like these using the SixX method, and then wait for answers. If the answers don't come right away, here's another trick: leave the question open and wait. You know when you're trying to remember something that's escaped you? If you try to force it, the answer doesn't come, but sometime later, the answer comes to mind. You can use this phenomenon when you feel out of ideas. When I'm stuck, I take a moment, think of the question I want to be answered, then take a break. I'll call a friend, do some stretches, take the dogs for a walk, or make dinner, and randomly, ideas will start coming to mind.

When I did my master's, there were a lot of people who struggled with a particular class that was famous for making students crazy. There was so much fear-mongering, warning us how hard this class would be, but also how important it was to our learning. Since I was starting to understand my relationship with my CTO, I realized these fears were counter-pro-ductive. If I told my CTO that doing this course was going to be hard and gruesome, then my CTO would oblige me. Why would I choose that?

This is how I taught myself work doesn't have to feel hard. Using the steps from the last chapter and this one, I created a goal statement and nicknamed my project "Easy A," then I created a staircase strategy with next steps, subgoals, and contingency plans (an activity you will do as part of your nitty-gritty plan). Did I have to do the work? Yup. But I chose to make doing the work feel light, fun, interesting, and to be excited about what I was learning. And that's exactly what came to pass.

Wrapping Up Brainstorming

You can wrap up a brainstorming session when it's evident that executing even a handful of your ideas would ensure success on your project. Ideally, you'll be patting yourself on the back and thinking how clever—and easy—some of these ideas of yours are.

It's just as important when you make a grand entrance to make a grand exit, as well. Meaning, how you finish a brainstorming session matters as much as how you start it. Do not cross out bad ideas. That's negative and backward looking, and as artist Mary Engelbreit famously said, "Don't look back—you're not going that way." Keep your focus on what you are going to do and not what you're not going to do. To finish a brainstorm, just ignore the things you're not going to do, and circle the things you are. It's that easy.

As you are circling ideas—and things feel more real—fear may crop up. Your CTO could well be on fire with resistance. Fear from your CTO sounds like, "That's going to be hard" or "I don't know how to do that." If this occurs, stay neutral, and even positive, as you tell your CTO, "Don't stress. Stay calm. We're going to know exactly how to crush these projects once we apply the nitty-gritty planning techniques that we are learning next."

Determine an Order of Operations

Your left hemisphere is going to be happy with this next task: taking all those fabulous ideas you just brainstormed and putting them in order as your subprojects. Your order of operations is not written in stone. You can and want to keep it flexible. The only subproject you want to do your best to identify correctly is the subproject you know you need to do next. Your first subproject needs to be so obvious you can't ignore it. It's that thing you need to accomplish, or you wouldn't forgive yourself for not trying. Once you select your first subproject, you will refer to it as your active assignment.

I know some of you will want to get a jump on two projects at once. After all, isn't two better than one? No. Resist the urge to overload your agenda with everything you've got. Focusing on one key project at a time is a counter-intuitive high-performance strategy. You will execute projects more swiftly and efficiently when you focus on one at a time. Choose an active assignment that you can't ignore, and as long as it is your active assignment, everything else you circled can wait.

Finalize Your Staircase Strategy

Creating a visual for your staircase strategy will make it feel more doable. Using a notepad or whiteboard, draw a staircase, and at the top, write down the nickname for your leap project. Then, on each of the descending steps, write down one major subproject you selected with your active assignment on the bottom step.

It's a rather fun activity with three big benefits. One, you will return to this staircase when you've completed your active assignment to choose your next project. Two, your CTO will love that it knows what's coming next and might even start working on some of your future projects in the background. Three, you've just established your major celebration milestones for your leap project. Each time you accomplish a step, it's time to celebrate.

Return to your staircase strategy and write down a reward next to each of the subprojects (steps) you identified. Once you've completed your staircase visual, you can move forward with the nitty-gritty planning for your active assignment.

Your Nitty-Gritty Plan

If your staircase strategy represented a series of pit stops you'd make on a road trip you were planning, your nitty-gritty plan would be your itinerary for what you planned to do during each stop. The value of planning is not that your plans work out exactly as you create them but that they groom your CTO for where you are headed. You only need to develop plans in great detail—or itineraries—for the subproject you are actively working on (your active assignment).

This might surprise you, but the first step for your active assignment is to create a goal statement using the MOMA Method mentioned in Chapter 7. You may have taken a considerable amount of time when you set your leap project goal statement and are worried about how much time this will take you. Setting goal statements for active assignments is easier. Once you get familiar with the MOMA Method, you will be able to create goal statements in under twenty minutes.

What comes after developing your goal statement? If you feel you are going up against a counter hot goal with this active assignment, then you will want to repeat the Chapter 7 activities for reprogramming your CTO. Once you have a MOMA goal statement and you've started the process for onboarding your CTO, you can move on to the brainstorming activity you just learned. Rinse and repeat. The only difference is this time, you'll be building on your brainstorm by following the additional steps below.

Mind Mapping

Nitty-gritty planning can become extensive. The process I teach my clients and program participants for planning active assignments is called mind mapping. It's a way to see, at one glance, the numerous ideas, steps, skills, tools, and resources you may need to achieve success. If you're not familiar with mind mapping, you can visit my resources page at https://www.jillmcabe.com/itsgotime_rabbit for an example. Also, unless you have tiny writing, a regular notebook isn't going to cut it. I recommend using the largest piece of paper you can get your hands on.

I use a flip chart or a whiteboard. If you don't have access to those, Bristol board or large unlined sketchbooks are available at most dollar stores. If you are someone who must work in a digital environment, while you should know that I think it's less desirable than working with pen and paper, there are free online tools that you can use for mind mapping as well.

The beginning of your nitty-gritty brainstorming is exactly like what you did to develop your staircase strategy. You start with conditional questions asking yourself how you might achieve your active assignment. You ask yourself these questions over and over, and remember to look for easier ways. Once you have followed these steps using a mind map, you can move on to the additional steps for nitty-gritty planning outlined here.

Empower Yourself with Behavioral Science

I've given you steps and tools for brainstorming, planning, and organizing, but that's just part of success. You've learned about the importance of your CTO and how, if not programmed correctly, all your planning can become derailed. Remember how your CTO gets programmed through repetition? Much of that repetition comes from your surroundings. If you want to become great with your time, then you need to understand the types of things that affect your actions. Behavioral science teaches us that how we live our lives is anything but free will. Until we take an active role in programming our CTOs, we are more like a pinball in the game of life.

One of the reasons I was successful at helping companies achieve turnarounds was not because I was some sort of natural genius (although let's not entirely rule that out); it was because I knew how to apply behavioral science by using what I knew, checklist-style, to the organization. My "mountain-moving" successes were possible because I had the right checklists, and they enabled me to control the factors that controlled the strings that controlled everything.

All I had to do was maintain the discipline to follow those checklists. I'm going to be giving you a checklist of things that, if you follow them, will make your success possible. When you follow these rules and develop nitty-gritty plans for your active assignments, you make success inevitable because you will control the conditions in your environment that control you. It's a powerful way of influencing yourself, and when you learn how to do it well, your CTO will be powerless to resist programming hot goals for anything you want.

Returning to the mind map you started, using the SixX method, take the following additional steps:

What Tools or Changes to Your Environment Could Help?

Ask yourself what tools could help you be more efficient. A few years ago, I worked on a computer with too little RAM. I was going crazy and dreamt of taking a baseball bat to my computer daily. I'd waste hours watching that spinning wheel. It was foolish. I had no respect for my time. Total false economy. The tools you need to complete your projects in a timely manner are not luxury items but necessities that will increase productivity.

Your physical environment also affects your performance. If you've ever tried to work in an open office space, and you're the kind of person who needs quiet to focus, then you know that your environment affects your productivity. One of my clients used to sit at her dining room table or on her living room couch with her laptop. When she finally put space aside in her home for an office, her productivity increased dramatically; she became organized, and even her family treated her work time more seriously. Make creating a space a part of your plan. If you don't have a good workspace, then creating one will be one of your first steps.

Remember how your CTO likes visual cues? Every project you are actively working on deserves a visual in your environment. Choose an image and place it somewhere prominent in your space to reinforce your success. Every time you walk by, you are programming your CTO. Like with the visual you chose to represent your leap project, pick an image or photo that motivates you. Even a sign with the nickname of your goal is a great start.

What Social Change Could Support You?

Humans are social creatures. We began our existence in tribes. Even with today's technology, we still have our people. The easiest way to figure out what you are likely to achieve is to simply look at your social environment. Whether or not you can see it, you are the average of the people you spend the most time with. If you don't like how much success you have, consider the people who are around you and what unspoken influences they have on your CTO.

If you don't like how much money you have, that has something to do with your circle of friends and family. This does not mean they are bad people; it just means their ambitions are not your ambitions, and therefore, there is a disconnect. One of the reasons I was so successful in my work in entrepreneurial organizations was that I understood this to be true and how to use this knowledge as a power to create positive change.

There's a phenomenon called the diffusion of innovation, originally developed by American communication theorist and sociologist Everett Rogers. Rogers is famous for his research showing that most people only try, buy, or do things once other people have tried, bought, or done those things first. You can use his insights to your advantage. When you understand that you subliminally copy the behavior of the people around you, all you need to do to improve any aspect of your life (or business) is spend more time with others who have achieved goals similar to the ones you now possess. When you do, you'll automatically start trying, buying, and doing things that will lead you to achieve your goals, just like they did.

What if you don't know anyone who has what you want? Try joining a group of people who are doing or have achieved what you want. Take small-group coaching programs with people who have similar goals to yours. Read biographies of people you admire. Watch TV shows about people you want to be like. Remember, your CTO can't tell the difference between real and imagined, so while you are building a real-life network of real people you admire, you can always start with research and entertainment to get you started.

What New Skills and Knowledge Do You Need?
As you are brainstorming all the things you could do to achieve your active assignment, you will probably discover a need for skills and knowledge you don't currently possess. You are progressing up the EBGM, which will steadily move you into territory that will require learning new things. In the explore phase, you may need to learn how to teach and coach adults,

create videos, position and market your program, and make sales. You will probably need to learn things like public relations, system development, money management, and team leadership skills in the exploit phase.

In case you're one of those people who likes to over-prepare, be mindful that you don't overdo this step and start learning things you don't need here and now. You only need to work on one thing at a time because you're only working on one active assignment at a time. For example, until you have a product you can lever into a business that you can grow or scale, don't clutter your mind with training about social media or marketing.

Unsubscribe and turn off your brain to everything that is not related to your active assignment. If there is an expert you want to follow up with when you hit a certain stage in your growth, then make a note of that somewhere, and return to them when you reach that phase.

Once you have considered the technical skills you need, explore what influence skills will make or break your success. You might know these skills as soft skills, a term that understates their importance. Influence skills are extremely beneficial. They cover areas like networking, negotiation, relationship building, selling your ideas, asking for help, and collaborating.

Influence skills separate people who achieve so-so results from those who achieve extraordinary ones. If you cannot influence yourself to follow your plan, you won't be successful. If you cannot influence others to work alongside you, join you on your journey, or work with you as a client, you'll never get out of the gate. They are the so-called soft skills that will give you hard-hitting results.

What Consequences Could Motivate You?

Although many people use consequences when planning, I learned in my change leadership work that there are far more effective ways to influence your CTO. Having said that, if consequences work for you, then include some.

If you want to motivate yourself with consequences for not succeeding at something, make sure the consequences are real. I've heard of one example where you give someone money to donate to a cause you are against if you miss a deadline. That wouldn't feel right to me, and I can't imagine my friends donating to a cause I was against.

Alex, a participant who took Ignite: Activate Your Big Idea, set up a hilarious consequence. He gave a good friend access to embarrassing pictures of himself. If he missed a deadline, she was to post one of the pictures on social media and tag him. Fun. (The last I checked, he was meeting all his deadlines!)

If you would like to use consequences to motivate you to stay on track with your plan, then think up some now that you believe you and your allies-in-success will follow through on.

What Rewards Could Motivate You?

Rewards can also help motivate you to see a plan through. I strongly urge you to set up rewards for as many subgoals as you can. I encourage fun and playful rewards because they tell your brain, "Hey, we're on the right track here." The more you reward yourself, the more you tell your CTO that what you're doing is desirable and that you want more of it. Positive reinforcement works on our pets ("Be a good puppy, and you get a treat!"), so why not try it on yourself? During your planning, be sure to brainstorm fifteen to twenty small and inexpensive or no-cost rewards you would enjoy. One of my favorite rewards is a dance party with my two dogs.

Wrapping up Nitty-Gritty Planning

At this point in your planning, you are probably looking at dozens to hundreds of ideas. Is your head spinning yet? The good news is you don't need to do them all. Instead, do what you did with your initial brainstorm, and circle the things you believe you need to move forward on. Then, sequence them in an order of operations that makes sense to you.

Set Deadline or Time Commitments

If you're a deadline lover, then you'll be happy that you've finally arrived at the step where you get to put dates and deadlines on your to-do list. Still, I have a caution. As I stressed in the previous chapter, if you set deadlines that aren't reasonable and you miss your deadlines, you are risking setting a hot goal for not following through on things.

An alternative to deadlines is to commit to times you will work toward your goal and get as much as possible done during that window. This involves deciding how many hours you will give a project, and then following through with the number you've committed to. Ranges are effective, too, because they give you latitude for when life happens. For example, I used both of these techniques while writing this book. In my planning, I committed to a range of five to six hours per day for as many days as I needed to complete my first draft. Also, my publisher had specific deadlines, and I needed to adhere to those strict timelines as well.

Patrick Was Better off with Time Commitments

Another Ignite participant, Patrick, was developing his plan to launch a new business and couldn't shake his pattern of setting unachievable deadlines. No matter what I taught, he'd keep submitting plans riddled with deadlines every few days. Patrick's attachment to deadlines worried me because I knew he'd struggled with procrastination since leaving his former job. I could also see he was falling behind the other participants in his group.

I implored Patrick to drop the deadlines and focus just on things he could control. I stressed how risky his approach was if he missed a single deadline due to his current, self-doubting state. Fortunately, he finally heard me and dropped the deadlines. In the following week, things started turning around for Patrick. He was full of enthusiasm and actively working on his goals. He later explained why he initially ignored my advice—every productivity course he'd ever taken before mine was big on deadlines.

Choose What Empowers You

Again, I'm not against deadlines. I'm not against consequences. I'm against deadlines and consequences that are at risk of not being followed through on because they have a destructive effect on your self-confidence and CTO. Real deadline pressure works wonders for productivity, and if you can create real deadline pressure, I wholeheartedly support using deadlines to get you working. False deadline pressure, on the other hand, backfires. It trains you to let yourself down and is a downright terrible idea for anyone struggling with their confidence or motivation.

Don't let frustration over where you are or excitement to move forward push you into setting unrealistic deadlines unless you are certain you will be able to honor them. Keep in mind your ability to honor deadlines will have everything to do with how experienced you are with the work you are about to engage in. We tend to be better at setting deadlines for things that we have done in the past than we are at setting deadlines for things that are brand new to us.

If you are not certain how long various tasks will take you to complete, then I urge you, like Patrick, to commit to ranges of time you know you can follow through on. Doing so will set you up to prove to your CTO that you've got what it takes to reach your new level of success. As we will explore in Chapter 10 on time practices, each time you follow through on a plan, you will get a hit of dopamine (a rewarding neurotransmitter) that will reinforce your CTO's instinct to continue working on that goal.

Whatever you decide, stick to it. This is where I agree with the productivity coaches who say you don't always need to be motivated. Force yourself to do whatever it takes to follow through on your promises to yourself. The more you get in the habit of following through, the more you will naturally follow through.

You're Almost Done!

If you are like my clients and program participants, you are probably itching to get moving on your project right now and tempted to put this book aside and get to work. After all, you've got your staircase strategy, which has given you a clear line of sight as to how you will achieve your leap project. You've identified an active assignment and created a nitty-gritty plan more detailed than any other you had before. You may well be wondering how on earth there can be anything more you need from the performance equation. If you are tempted to get started right now, I urge you to resist the temptation and press on with the next piece of the puzzle: how to prepare to win when passing through challenging terrain

CHAPTER 9:

Prepare for Challenging Terrain

I n my experience, when pursuing ambitious goals, you can count on circumstances arising that will threaten your success. In this chapter, you will learn planning techniques to succeed at projects where you have little or no prior experience. You will achieve this by predicting foreseeable obstacles, pre-determining how you will overcome them, and onboarding your CTO. After that, you will learn about making space for new activities by eliminating things in your life that no longer serve you. We'll close the chapter by delving into the power of deciding and exploring a new perspective toward challenges that will empower you.

How to Zip around Obstacles

You're probably familiar with contingency planning. The idea is to identify predictable obstacles and pre-determine how you will overcome them. We will do that here, and we will take it one step further. If you want to zip around obstacles as a Ferrari would, the best way to accomplish that is to program your CTO to do just that.

Even when you foray into the unknown, there are two types of circumstances that you can expect. The first are the obstacles you can predict with reasonable accuracy because similar situations have thwarted your progress in the past. The second are the random distractions that pop up: the predictable, unpredictable events that are part of life. We'll use contingency planning to overcome both.

How to Overcome Predictable Obstacles

As I understood better how my brain worked, I realized that programming myself to overcome predictable frustrating events in my life was going to be incredibly liberating.

I started small. I used to routinely misplace personal items—things like my phone, wallet, keys, and umbrellas. Of course, each time it happened, I ended up wasting time and running late. It was a predictable obstacle I was ready to put in my past. I realized that if I had this problem, I must have set up a hot goal to misplace items . . . or run late. Either way, I decided to program a new hot goal to always know where my items were.

To reprogram my CTO, I used visuals to illustrate my new goal. I also conveyed that this change to my usual pattern would bring me happiness and peace of mind. I was being seated in a restaurant when I had this epiphany. It was raining that day, and I had just placed my umbrella under a chair as an automatic thought popped into my head: "I hope I don't leave it here." I thought this because until that point in my life, if I brought an umbrella to a restaurant, and it was not raining when I left, I was almost sure to leave it behind.

A Peculiar Hot Goal

Sometime during my life, I had programmed my CTO, Samantha, to forget umbrellas. Odd but true. I started working on programming a hot goal to remember umbrellas from that point forward. First, I wondered why I forgot them and realized it was because when there was no rain to trigger my CTO to get my umbrella, it was easy to forget. I realized I needed to create new triggers for my CTO, which had nothing to do with the weather. I considered all the events that took place right before I needed to grab my umbrella, so I could condition my CTO to step up to the plate when I needed her to.

Then I closed my eyes and pictured myself going through the motions of finishing my lunch, paying, standing up, putting on my jacket, picking up my purse, and then, critically, looking under the table to see if there was anything else. Furthermore, I pictured myself feeling the positive emotion of gratification as I remembered to take my umbrella. Then I opened my eyes, explained my peculiar behavior to my lunch date and enjoyed my lunch.

To my delight, it worked. Just as I put my purse over my shoulder, I had an instinct to look under the table for anything else, and there was my umbrella. I nearly skipped down the street as I realized the implications of this. I could reprogram myself for success for anything I could predict, as long as I managed to figure out effective triggers to call my CTO to attention. Over the months that followed, I reprogrammed my CTO to remember the locations of all my important personal items, and now my self-talk in this regard is that I always know the location of my important things.

Contingency Planning with a Hot Goal

As silly as it is, the example above is no different than anything you can predict might happen to you. If you can predict spending too much time on social media, playing games, or watching Netflix, you can overcome them just the way I did. The following activity will walk you through the steps used to reprogram your CTO when it comes to overcoming predictable obstacles.

What Obstacles Can You Predict?

Thinking of your active assignment, ask yourself, "What is the most likely thing to go wrong?" It's easy for most people to answer this. This is a question you're going to want to ask three to five times, but not with the

SixX method you use in some of the other activities. This is in case you have a highly creative CTO who is an expert at thinking up borderline absurd possibilities. The goal is not to invite your CTO to drum up absurd answers or to answer the question, "What is every imaginable thing that might go wrong?" Stay focused on the words "most likely." This is what we are concerned with here and how to succeed with this activity.

Once again, starting with possibilities before decisions, for each likely obstacle you identified, ask yourself, "How might I be able to overcome that? How else? How else?" Once you've got a compelling list of ideas that you believe will work, review your list, circle your favorites, and proceed to onboarding your CTO.

Convert Your Overcome Plans to Hot Goals

As in the case with my umbrella, when you want to program a hot goal to overcome a situation you can predict, you want to include a trigger that will remind your CTO to execute the actions you're asking for. To achieve this, complete this statement as it pertains to your situation: "If/when [possible obstacle] happens, I will [describe the steps you will follow to overcome the obstacle]." Then close your eyes and imagine yourself encountering the possible obstacle, any specifics about the situation you can predict, the steps you decided on, and, critically, the positive emotions you will feel as you prevail.

How to Overcome Surprise Obstacles

Let's take a look at the second type of situation: real surprises. There are those surprise jobs for clients that come with a big paycheck. There is the burst water pipe in your basement. There's the friend who gets ill who you want to support. These are the things that are not necessarily predictable and fall into the category of "life happens." They are the unexpected events that threaten to steal from the time you blocked out to work on your active assignment.

One of the hardest surprise obstacles to overcome for people who work for themselves is the allure of a juicy gig that's not quite in your wheelhouse. By "juicy," I mean you get offered a nice chunk of cash or a job with a prestigious client. By "not in your wheelhouse," I mean it's not what you usually do, so it will take you a disproportionate amount of your time and focus to deliver great work.

If you are faced with an opportunity such as this—one that requires you to steal from your twenty percent leap-project time—should you take it? The answer depends on whether you believe the project will move you closer to the vision of your life you're working toward in a way you didn't predict.

More often than not, I hear stories of clients who took offers they shouldn't have because there was no long-term gain. The money they made came and went with expenses that somehow arose to consume it. The job didn't lead to a steady stream of referrals because it wasn't quite what they usually do, and worse, their clients were unusually demanding and time consuming to serve.

Use Your Happiness Recipe

To make the decision that's right for you, go back to your Happiness Recipe from Chapter 5 and use it as your decision guide. Consider whether saying yes will move you in the direction of your pathfinder vision. Will it be an expression of your purpose? Will it be in harmony with your values? If you answer yes to all three, then great. It's a good project for you.

If not, I urge you to resist the temptation to detour from your plan. There's a famous bar sign that says, "Free beer tomorrow." Of course, tomorrow never comes, and you won't magically find the time to build a business you love running tomorrow either. One of the reasons I was finally able to build a business that's perfect for me is I learned how to say no to opportunities that took me off course.

I could have built my business even faster had I stopped chasing short-term cash sooner. In my case, I used to agree to give seminars that were in my area of expertise but were not in my catalog. I love leading live training and the topics I'd be asked to speak about, but developing custom curriculums takes time. I realized the folly of my ways on one particular job that offered me a tantalizing paycheck for a three-hour session. How could I say no?

It turns out I should have. I ended up prepping that session for weeks to ensure happy clients. They were thrilled, but that fancy paycheck didn't add up to much per hour. Had I spent the same amount of time developing a new course for Skillshare, I would have bolstered my passive income every month and simultaneously established a lead generation tool that could attract new students to BOOM-U.

When surprise obstacles pop up that threaten to pull you away from your plan, whether a juicy gig, an invitation to go sailing, or an urgent need from a family member or a friend, ask yourself: can you squeeze it into your 80 percent time block? Or are you going to steal from your 20 percent? Go back to your Happiness Recipe. If the diversion aligns with the pathfinder vision you established for yourself, then go for it. Otherwise, turn it down.

Getting Real about What's Not Working

In 2015, I went to a meditation retreat in Carlsbad, California offered by internationally-recognized meditation teacher Davidji. His retreat was focused around setting one primary intention for the year and how to use meditation as a tool to make our intentions happen.

At the time, I had been practicing change leadership in organizations for years, so even back then, it was rare that I would learn anything new about planning. I was surprised when Davidji offered a fresh idea, one that is implicit throughout the change field but that was far more powerful when Davidji made it explicit.

Davidji explained that for everything we want to bring into our lives, there is something we need to give up to make room for it. He gave the example of needing to get rid of your old couch if you want a new one. He had us make a list of things that were not serving our lives and plan for how we would rid ourselves of them. The closing of the activity brought it home as we turned to our partners, with hands on our hearts, and committed to following through.

It was a potent activity, and I knew there was no going back on the promise I made on that day. I've come to learn just how important releasing what isn't working is when you want more success. To me, even the title of this book, *It's Go Time*, is as much about getting somewhere better as it is about leaving what's not working behind.

What's Got to Go?

When it comes to thinking of what needs to go in your life, I invite you to think beyond your active assignment and leap project to thinking more broadly about your Happiness Recipe. Take a few minutes to reacquaint yourself with your purpose acorn, the pathfinder vision you created for three years from now, and your updated, empowering values, and then ask yourself what has to go.

The answers that are likely to arise are any combination of physical things you need to get rid of or replace, unproductive activities that are not serving you, and relationships that are holding you back.

Physical things you need to let go of are by far the easiest of the three categories to deal with. Whether it's your office chair that's leading to lower back pain or your phone that's so old you lose hours each week waiting for it to unfreeze or restart, once you make the decision that it's high time to change it, you'll probably cross that item off your list pretty quickly.

The next category is unproductive activities—binge-watching Netflix, playing video games for hours on end, excessive scrolling on social media, obsessing over being perfect, and taking too long on projects. Saying goodbye to activities you spend time on is harder because whatever you are doing is currently related to a hot goal. If you have activities that fall into this category, be prepared to create a full-on subproject (starting with a MOMA goal statement and following through to a nitty-gritty plan) to achieve your desired change.

The majority of my clients are challenged by the idea of addressing their limiting social ties. Whether it's people that you've known for years who, although well-meaning, are out of sync with you because they have no urge to grow themselves or those who are straight-up draining to be around, it can be difficult to stop seeing people who've been a part of your life for a long time.

What Relationships Aren't Working?

If there are people you are spending time with and you don't want to be like them or they don't make you feel like you can be your most authentic version of yourself, you need to think about why you're spending time with them. If you stay around people you don't want to be like, you're dramatically reducing, if not eliminating, your chances of reaching the level of success you are after. The laws of social assimilation are more powerful than you can probably imagine.

But what if the people who are draining you are your family? What do you do then?

A program participant, Andrew, had a draining relationship with his parents. Andrew did not believe he could "fire his parents from his life" as he put it, yet every time he saw them, which was once every two weeks, their negative emotional wake would bring him down for days. Almost all they did was complain—complain about politics, about their neighbors, about each other, and about him. The one positive thing they liked to talk about was how successful Andrew's cousins were. He couldn't take it.

Andrew felt a duty to his parents and didn't want to limit his family visits without trying other methods. He decided to talk to them about his needs. Andrew told them that he did not respond well to their negativity and their sky-is-falling view of the world. He told them he felt depressed after seeing them and asked them to find positive things to talk about during his visits. He told them he'd reduce his visits if they couldn't find ways to be more optimistic in his presence. Remarkably, things got much better, just based on that one talk.

I've had other clients "save" relationships with effective heart-to-heart talks, but overall, the more you spend time with family or friends who are not on the same trajectory as you or don't bring out the best in you, the more you are likely to delay your success.

Onboarding Your CTO with What's Gotta Go

Once you've decided what things, activities, and relationships need to go (or be reduced), follow the same steps to start programming new hot goals as you did with your contingency plans. Start with possibilities for how you will make these changes, decide what you are going to move forward with, and then translate your decision into a language your CTO understands by imagining yourself encountering the temptations and situations you want to limit and how you will behave differently. Add power to this activity by imagining how good choosing to work toward your pathfinder vision will make you feel.

What Should Success Feel Like?

I once attended a panel to hear three entrepreneurs talk about how they built their businesses. All three were first-time entrepreneurs and doing well. During the Q&A, a member of the audience asked how they knew their businesses were the right ones for them. They unanimously agreed; their business success came easily to them, which is how they knew they were on the right track.

I reflected on how at odds their perspective was with the advice we often hear: if you want something meaningful, be prepared to work hard for it. Failure is to be expected on the road to success, so be resilient, learn from mistakes, and keep going until you get there. Fall seven times; get up eight.

Do you agree with the three entrepreneurs from the panel that if something's meant for you, success will come easily? To help you decide, picture yourself three years from now with all the goals you'd set for yourself accomplished. You're at a party with friends, and you're telling the story of how you made it all happen, how easy it all was. Once you created your plan, everything fell into place. Better yet, imagine someone telling you a story about their magic carpet ride to success. Would you be hanging onto every word or wondering if you should go home and do your laundry?

The Story You Probably Want to Tell

When I talk to my clients and program participants once they achieve the goals they established when working with me, you know what stories they enjoy sharing the most? They enjoy talking about their hard-won successes, the obstacles that got in the way, and the factors that arose against them . . . but how they did it anyway.

If you're like most of the people I work with, then you wouldn't like the version of you that had all of your successes handed to you. Success tastes sweeter when you decide nothing will stop you. As my former client Janet Zuccarini said after going from being an unknown owner of a single restaurant in Toronto to a television personality and an award-winning owner of a multinational restaurant group, "My overnight success was years in the making."

When my clients and program participants start working with me, some of them are so frustrated and ready for a win that they've become sensitive to setbacks. This is a natural response when repeated past attempts to elevate their working situation didn't work out.

Here's what you need to decide for yourself. Even with the all-in system you are learning here, and even with your budding relationship with your CTO, you can expect to encounter frustrations and setbacks. I ask you, will you do it anyway?

Decide and Commit

It's vital at this point in the process that you commit to following through on your pathfinder vision, leap project, and active assignment. Genuine commitment has a powerful emotional energy that can reprogram your CTO in an instant. Will you only go after your dreams if they come quickly and easily, or are you willing to be all-in until you succeed?

If you tell yourself you will only do this if it comes quickly and easily, you will almost certainly give up too soon. This is true of any goal you set for yourself; if you're not all-in, you're almost certain to give up before you had any chance of succeeding. You have a chance now to make a decision that will change your life.

Several people I've helped are on the brink of giving up when they find me. A story I've heard several versions of is as follows: A heart-centered talented person (or partners) put a course online. They spent months creating the material and developing the curriculum. They get a few students who get incredible results but are stressed out because they can't figure out how to make a decent living with it. Not knowing what their problem is, they change their positioning. Months later, their new positioning doesn't lead to sales, so they change their positioning again. Again, it doesn't take, and once again, they try again.

When people in this situation come to me, their lack of follow-through is a big part of their problem. It takes a year or more to get known for a topic when following a comprehensive system. When you select your projects, do so with care. Commit to a target market first. Then, commit to being a scrappy explorer and not building your program, experience, or solution without beta or case study clients that have bought into your idea.

Mitigating the Risk Can Be the Risk

I'll admit this is not only the story of some of my clients. Several years ago, I discovered the difference between wanting a goal badly and making an all-in commitment. I had been working toward my dream business for years, and my progress had been slow. Financially, I needed to decide whether I would continue or return to my former work as a vision and strategy consultant.

My bank account said it was time to give up, but I knew I had created something special. After some deep soul-searching, I realized I had been doing too much DIY. I was playing small to mitigate my risk. Then it dawned on me; mitigating my risk was the risk. From that point on, I decided to be all-in, making tough decisions as though I was guaranteed success.

In my case, going all-in turned out to be expensive! I did things like upgrade my conferences to VIP and sought out experts in my field that offered small group environments over those en-mass group coaching programs I had been taking. In the span of about four months, I had invested $105,000 in my business.

Although it challenged me, I was willing to make this investment in my business because I had a decade of glowing testimonials, proof of concept, and positioning; I just needed leverage. Although I had no guarantee my investment would pay off, deep down, I felt at peace because what mattered to me was that I was showing up for myself with everything I had.

We love our guarantees and insurances, the promises that everything will turn out well and we will be safe. Except, the need for safety, assurances, and guarantees keep us from going all-in on our goals, which in turn, reduces the likelihood we'll stick with them long enough to succeed.

Finding Faith and Following Through

I have come to learn over the years that tools, training, systems, tips, and tricks will fall short unless you bring ingredients only you can bring, faith and follow through.

Laurie Anne King is an intuitive coach and portrait photographer who had been in business for thirty years when she joined Basecamp. Until that point, her primary business offerings were one-on-one sessions and spiritual photo shoots. When she joined Basecamp, the COVID-19 situation had unexpectedly forced her to close the doors to her portrait studio for a period of time.

During Basecamp, she developed her signature program, *Open Inward to Eternal Wisdom*. Even with our team and me right by her side, her journey was not an easy one. Despite Laurie Anne being gifted at what she does, deep down, she needed to find more faith in herself. Here's what she wrote about the journey of creating her signature program and finding her faith.

Creating Open Inward to Eternal Wisdom

In a former life, I was under the illusion that I was running a good business, effectively sharing my gifts with the world. I have the advantage of a loyal client base that kept me under the impression I was doing rather well.

In reality, I was not serving my clients in the highest way possible, and I was closed off to this fact until the COVID-19 situation caused me to re-evaluate my situation. When I took Basecamp with Jill, the penny finally dropped.

The truth is what I was doing was blindly staying small and not doing or knowing how to do the specific personal work to reach my next level of potential. No one can do it for you. This is true. What is also true is that we need each other to reach our potential. We can't thrive being an island.

Before taking the time to develop a signature program with Jill, I spent an enormous amount of time and resources working on my business with a DIY mentality, believing I could not afford to do it any other way. I was getting small rewards for big effort, but at least I was consistent. But seriously, cracking the self-delusional code of what was holding me back was a massive awakening.

A familiar internal battle with a cynical and distrustful voice in my head was working hard to convince me that the system I was learning from Jill wouldn't work for me. Would a signature program really make that much of a difference? In truth, I was feeling the kind of relief that happens when much-needed help arrives on the scene. My wheels had fallen off long ago.

Thankfully, my YES answer pushed through the distractions I had created to protect my small and familiar reality from change. It is strange how we resist change when it always brings renewal to our lives. The first sobering thing I learned was that I was deficient in my faith around my gifts.

There were many more revelations to follow. My whole journey of creating Open Inward to Eternal Wisdom was challenging me in areas I'd never challenged myself before. But it was worth it. The results were nothing short of liberat-

ing. I mean, dancing around my living room kind of liberating! "I can do this. OMG, this is happening!"

I had barely finished Basecamp, and I already had a fully booked out signature program. My head was spinning at the results. Suddenly, money was pouring into my bank account from folks who had faith in me. I had to pinch myself. I knew I could never have gotten there without pushing through my internal barriers.

It was clear that I needed to roll up my sleeves if I wanted results, and I did. It was up to me and I followed through. I created something I never anticipated—I now teach people how to develop their psychic gifts. My students are getting incredible results. My program is getting continued enrolment, and I have a new vision for my lifestyle and increasing financial security. Woot Woot!

It's funny, but as I reread what I just wrote, I say out loud to myself, "Far out." You know, even now, as I reflect on this journey that is still so fresh, I am amazed I got here! When we have the right tools for the job, we can achieve great things. The system you are learning is solid. You will have to do the work, though. I am thrilled to say I came out on the other side with flying colors, and I am quite proud of myself. Have faith and you will come out the other side, too.

Tell Your Hero's Tale

Do you know what the hero's journey is? The hero's journey is a storyline used in entertainment because it's so alluring. The hero's journey starts with a reasonably fast rise to success, but there's a crisis that brings the hero down to what appears to be rock bottom. Then, they start to climb back up, but along the way, they hit another obstacle and their true rock bottom. Finally, things start looking up, their path is fraught with small trials, but before they know it, their life is better than they ever imagined it would be.

Starting with the premise that you are a hero, have already hit your second rock bottom, and are now on your hilly but certain climb to success, take a few minutes to imagine yourself in your future with your pathfinder vision achieved. Have a look around at what your business is like and what that has allowed you to do in your life. Picture the people in your life your success has had a positive impact on and how they have benefited. Now, create a story about how you achieved all this, complete with the ups and downs you experienced. Use these triggers to add depth to your story:

- A surprise obstacle and how you overcame it
- Old goal(s)/beliefs that you reprogrammed
- The skills you acquired
- The new people in your life and what these relationships are like
- Any further nitty-gritty (even fun) details you can think of

Talk to a Mentee

Now imagine you are talking to a young person who is in the situation you are in now. They have a dream—the exact dream you have now—and they are asking you to tell them how you succeeded so they know what to expect. What advice will you give them? Will you encourage them to go for it or dissuade them because of the risk?

What Did You Decide?

When I ask my clients and program participants how it felt for them to imagine their hero's journeys, they usually tell me it felt a bit stressful and upsetting. When I ask my clients what advice they gave their mentees, they unanimously tell their mentees that even if there are bumps in the road, they should do it anyway.

It's Time for You to Decide

I've given you a lot of time to think about what you want for your future and what you want your leap project to be to get you there. I would be doing you a disservice if I let you turn the page without having you make a commitment to what you will follow through on. It doesn't matter if you don't commit to all of it right now; what matters is that whatever you commit to is what you do.

You have an opportunity right now to make a true commitment, a vow. Make that vow, and commit to using this rinse-and-repeat performance equation on the subsequent projects and subprojects ahead of you, and you can expect success. If you're ready to commit, put your hand on your heart and state your commitment out loud. If you have someone who fully supports you in your life, make the commitment to them the next time you see them, and ask them to respond with the words, "I believe in you."

You get to decide how much or how little you will commit to, and remember, what you genuinely commit to is what you will do.

You Are Well Prepared

In this chapter, you learned how to plan to succeed at projects even if, like Laurie Anne King, you're starting out with a little doubt. You have learned how to anticipate and surmount both predictable and unpredictable events that are a part of life. You took a good look at limiting elements of your environment, activities, and relationships that drain you. You stepped back from your planning and took a good look at what you can expect your journey to success to be like. You started exploring your hero's journey.

You'll be amazed at how quickly your life starts to change when you take your plans to this level. Each step you take moves you toward your bigger dreams and builds your confidence. In turn, you continue to raise the bar for yourself. Your world is perfectly organized for the results you're currently getting. By completing Phase III, you now know the science of rearranging your world to get any results you want.

In Phase IV, the rubber meets the road. You now know what you're going to do, why you want to do it, and how you will. It's time to turn to learning daily and weekly practices that will help you get more accomplished in less time, the final elements of your performance equation.

Phase IV:

Practices to Speed Up Ascension

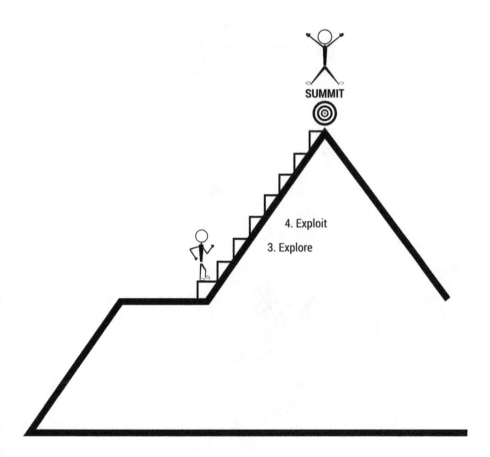

CHAPTER 10:

The Dopamine Drip

You have truly earned the right to start thinking about how to organize your days. You've gotten clear about what you care about and what you want. You've created a Happiness Recipe; you've identified a purpose acorn, created a pathfinder vision, and established values that will become your future hot goals. You've selected a leap project and a strategy staircase you know you could execute. You've identified an active assignment and created a nitty-gritty plan so detailed it would make a business school professor blush. There's nothing left to do but review how to raise your game when it comes to your productivity.

In academia, performance is repeatedly measured by an individual's level of motivation multiplied by their level of ability; that is, motivation x ability = performance. You've already got the skills (ability) of your trade. In this book, you have developed your ability to pick better projects, onboard your CTO with hot goals, and create winning plans. In this chapter, we will fill in the final piece of the performance equation: practices that intrinsically motivate you and thus take you from prepared to unstoppable.

Can you even influence your motivation? According to the work of Harvard Business School professor Teresa Amabile and her colleague, author Steven J. Kramer, summarized in their Harvard Business Review article, "The Power of Small Wins," published in the May 2011 issue, you can.

In their research on what motivated knowledge workers (people who sell their talent and time in organizations), Amabile and Kramer dispelled a once-popular belief that a pat on the back for a job well-done is the most effective way to motivate individuals. As it turns out, that is not accurate and can even feel demotivating at times. According to their research, a sense of progress toward a meaningful goal is more motivating. Amabile and Kramer demonstrated that, in organizations, the way to capitalize on this is to make sure knowledge workers are working toward a meaningful goal and recognize progress every step of the way.

Not only does their finding feel like common sense, Amabile and Kramer's discovery is also consistent with modern neuroscience. Assuming a goal is meaningful, thereby also a hot goal, then regular action toward it would be rewarding, and, more importantly, would release regular doses of dopamine.

A Positively Reinforcing Cycle

Dopamine is a chemical produced by the body that generates feelings of reward and pleasure. It influences the activities your CTO chooses to spend time on. Your CTO seeks out actions and activities that release dopamine into your system. Whenever you are doing anything at all (whether it's what you think you ought to be doing or not), you are doing whatever will produce the greatest amount of dopamine for you at that moment.

When my clients and program participants first learn this, they are sometimes disheartened. They find it hard to believe that procrastinating or spending too much time online or watching Netflix could ever be their best way to get dopamine. When you choose to spend time on an activity you don't find fulfilling over something you believe would make your

The Dopamine Drip | 161

situation better, there is sure to be a limiting hot goal behind your CTO's action. I encourage you not to worry if you are not naturally choosing projects that are important to you.

Instead, I invite you to think about how you can capitalize on the irresistible power of the dopamine drip by following Amabile and Kramer's advice and steadily reminding yourself of all the progress you are making toward your goals, no matter how small. If you do, eventually working on the projects you feel are important will become better sources of dopamine than those procrastination habits and distractions you've been trying to ditch!

Time Practices

What you will learn in this chapter are a series of daily and weekly activities that either prime your brain to work on a given task or increase the frequency with which you reward yourself with dopamine. Hand-in-hand, the activities you learn here will become a positive reinforcing cycle. The longer you do them, the easier they will become and the more natural progress toward your goal will feel.

This chapter is not about having you micromanage your life. Instead, it shares practices that will groom your CTO to get more dopamine for working on the projects that are important to you and less dopamine for your hot goals that are out-of-date. Continued use of these practices will lead to the hot goals you've been working on becoming hotter. Use these practices for a month or two, and the practices themselves will become hot goals, which will establish a positive reinforcing cycle that will lead to you instinctively getting the right work done and becoming unstoppable. You will learn:

- Morning Practice: To speed up the reprogramming of your CTO
- End-of-Day Practice: A daily recap that will help you create better to-do lists
- Bedtime: A nighttime activity that increases your motivation and sense of self

- Weekly Reviews: A weekly recap to keep you focused on your top priorities
- Prep-to-Work Practices: High-performance practices to do more in less time
- Pinch-Hit Practice: How to learn and become competent and do anything faster

Time Management Is a Misnomer

Before I share these practices with you, please stop using the phrase "time management." It's a misleading concept, and because of that, I believe it contributes to people struggling to make the most of their time.

The Google definition for "management" is "the process of dealing with or controlling things or people." I think it's fair to say that it is impossible to control time. I suppose you could say that we "deal with time," but this is a slightly depressing concept.

I will not go through my life thinking about it as something I need to deal with, and I hope you reject that notion as well. Time is more like money; it's something you can invest and spend wisely. To me, time is well spent when I look back on what I've done and think, "Heck, yeah. I wouldn't change a thing."

As you move forward, I invite you to use the phrase "time practices." When you practice something enough, your CTO will eventually do the lion's share of the work. Practice is how to make your life easier. Practice is how to take something from a point that requires effort to a point where it's easy. It's what you do that eventually leads to habits. When you start introducing better practices into your day-to-day routines, you set in motion events that make your life better and better from now on.

SOP: Make Time Your Partner

If you've ever worked in a larger organization, you might consider what I teach you in this chapter as an SOP (standard operating procedure) for time. In case you're not familiar with the term SOP, it stands for a set of steps you follow each time you approach a specific procedure or task. Company policy is to always follow those steps in order.

This SOP provides a structure that takes the guesswork out of your planning. It gives you a logical framework for how to allocate time, use it to your advantage, and choose your work effectively. When you follow these steps, you'll be able to look back on the week, month, and year, and think to yourself, "Heck, yeah. I'm proud of how I've lived."

I had a hard time deciding which part of this SOP to start you with (morning review, evening review, or weekly review) because all of the activities that follow are interdependent. I made the arbitrary decision to start with mornings, but the system won't fully come together until you read through all daily and weekly practices.

Mornings Practice: Programming Your CTO
Earlier in the book, I introduced you to a practice I called Thinking Vitamins so you could start onboarding your CTO. Now that you have a leap project and active assignment identified, I would like you to progress to Morning Thinking Vitamins to be used as part of your morning routine. If you would like a printout of these, you can get one at https://www. jillmcabe.com/itsgotime_rabbit.

Starting each day with Morning Thinking Vitamins is an inspiring way to get connected with your CTO after sleep, and it will kickstart your first dopamine release of the day. If you make an effort to also visualize what you are thinking about and connect to positive emotions while you are doing them, you'll get even more benefit from the activity. As before, I suggest you do Morning Thinking Vitamins while lying in bed or brushing your teeth:
- My purpose (acorn/sapling or tree) is …
- My leap project is connected to my purpose (acorn) because …
- My active assignment on my leap project is …
- Three or more awesome things that will happen if I achieve my active assignment are …

- This will be good for other people (clients, family, collaborators) in my life because …
- Three or more reasons I have what it takes to achieve my active assignment are …
- Even if I encounter setbacks, I can achieve my active assignment anyway because …
- Three or more things I am grateful for about my current situation (business and life) are …
- I can and will bring joy as I work toward my goals today because …

After your Morning Thinking Vitamins, take a quick look at the to-do list you created the night before. (I show you how to do your evening to-do list in the next activity.)

How Early Do You Need to Rise?

Before we move on to your evening time practices, I'll take a moment to address the idea out there that you have to be a morning person to be successful. Google is full of examples of successful people who start their day early—and I mean 3:45 a.m. and 4:30 a.m. early. Since it's the Internet, you can find just as many articles debunking this concept. Where do we find the truth?

When I ran JOV Bistro, an inventor, who I'll call Fred, used to come in and have dinner almost every Wednesday. He would sit at the bar and talk to us while we polished glassware. Fred invented part of the technology that enables us to pay with debit cards, so yeah, he's pretty successful. I had dozens of conversations with Fred over the years.

I'll never forget Fred telling me that he wakes up at 10:00 a.m. most mornings and works until the wee hours. He pointed out that people have their rhythm, and what's most important about being productive is honoring your rhythm. If you're a morning person, great. Enjoy that. But if you're not, then remember Fred, the multimillionaire who wakes up at 10:00 a.m. or later each day. He hasn't let other people's theories and opinions shame him into acting against his wishes. Disregard all of the talk telling you to be someone other than who you are. Focus on when you do your best work, then build your schedule around that.

End of Day Practice: Your Tomorrow's To-Dos

At the end of each workday, review what you accomplished and create a list for what you intend to accomplish the following day. Most high achievers put more on each day's list than is reasonable to accomplish in a given day. If you do this, please don't give yourself a hard time for things you didn't do or even cross anything out. When you are hard on yourself, you diminish your productivity over time. Instead, I encourage you to put a checkmark next to the items you achieved and a little forward arrow (→) in front of any item you will reschedule for another day.

One thing I like when it comes down to my daily list is an idea that David Allen shared in his book, *Getting Things Done*. Allen distinguishes the language of tasks versus projects. He said projects take multiple steps to achieve, and tasks can be done with a single action. He has you write your to-do list for each day with only tasks on it.

For example, I might have the project to review my quarterly profit and loss, and there would be several tasks toward that, including "download bank statements" and "send bookkeeper bank statements." Another brain-friendly piece of advice from Allen is that you should always write down tasks starting with a verb because it makes it easier for your brain to warm up to doing them. I have used it for several years and agree that it's a terrific productivity hack.

Finally, on every day's to-do list, I include at least one activity, usually two, that regenerates me; even if it's just walking the dogs for an hour or taking a fitness break, it gets written down.

Bedtime Practice: Happygrams for Motivation

When I helped my mom move out of her country home, I found these cute little slips of paper in a small box labeled "Happygrams." I asked her what they were. She used to run a remedial education school, helping kids with learning differences, like the ones I had. In the conventional school system, her students were used to notes being sent home detailing what was wrong. My mom decided to send her students home with notes celebrating their progress.

Amabile and Kramer would have been impressed by my mom, who decades before these individuals conducted their groundbreaking research on motivation, recognized her students' small wins. What a smart mom I have!

I create a Happygram for myself every evening before I go to sleep. It gives me my evening dopamine fix. I suggest you do the same. No matter how you feel about your day, no matter if it was the worst or the best day you've ever had, recount and detail everything you can think of that you did well, appreciated, or feel grateful for that day.

To create my Happygrams, I complete the phase, "Today I'm happy about ..." And then I use the SixX method to make a laundry list of everything I can think of. Don't limit Happygrams to work situations. I include anything about my day that I am happy I did and even things that happened to me. It could be about my work, fitness, friends, or family. It all belongs on my Happygram.

Ignoring your positive actions and things you appreciate about your life, regardless of how fleeting or insignificant they may appear, cheats your CTO out of getting extra hits of dopamine for the things that are going well in your life. Conversely, exaggerating things that didn't go well is destructive and will diminish your ability and motivation over time.

In practice, this means if you spent the day in bed because you were unwell, congratulate yourself for getting the rest you needed. If you spent today clearing off your desktop because it was distracting you, then you give yourself credit for setting up your workspace. If you tried to work and it just wasn't coming, then you give yourself credit for taking the break you needed to allow the ideas to flow to you. And since you're reading this book today, give yourself a Happygram during your evening recap for investing in your professional development.

Giving yourself credit for every lick of progress you make is an easy win and a smart thing to do. When you focus on the progress you're making, no matter how small, you're telling your CTO you've done something that promotes your wellbeing. This, in turn, will release more dopamine. If you commit to nightly Happygrams, you will install a positive self-reinforcing cycle that will put you on the fast track to becoming unstoppable.

Weekly Reviews: Increasing Your Ongoing Focus
I like to do my weekly reviews on Sunday afternoons right before dinner. Some people prefer to carve out the last hour or two of their Fridays. If you're not sure what would be better for you, try both, then choose the time that fits. For my weekly reviews, I first reflect on the week gone by, then I create a big picture plan for the week ahead.

Reviewing the Week Gone By
I ask myself the following questions for the weekly review, but I do not journal these answers. I just take about ten minutes to look at my list from the previous week and contemplate how I did.
- What were my goals from last/this week? ("This week," if you do yours on Friday.)
- What were my wins and highlights from last/this week?
- One or more times I was most proud of myself last/this week were ...
- A way I limited myself during last/this week was ...
- A lesson I learned last/this week was ...

You'll notice that part of this weekly review feels like a Happygram when you document your wins, highlights, and times you were most proud of yourself. Again, this is important for your CTO and dopamine. Every time you think of progress—and feel good about it—you are reinforcing your desirable hot goals.

You can see the idea is not to be delusional because you will give attention to whether or not you limited yourself and lessons you learned. Reviews are not about ignoring reality. The key point is not to fret if you didn't get to everything you hoped to do, but rather to get real with yourself. In my case, I am notorious for over-planning. What I am looking for is productivity. Did I work on my most important goals? Did I allow distractions to control my attention? If I was productive, great. If not, okay, no judgment. If I feel there is room to improve my productivity, I simply do an activity I will share with you later in this chapter called Keep, Stop, Start.

Planning the Week Ahead

Once I have finished my review for the week gone by, I turn my attention to what I want to accomplish in the week ahead. I make a laundry list of everything I would like to accomplish in the week to come. I call this a laundry list because I will almost certainly include more projects and tasks than I will have time to get done. My final step is to prioritize my list to communicate with my CTO what I want to achieve most.

I wrap up my weekly review by creating my specific to-do plan for Monday. (As a reminder, include something that regenerates you.) Then I put my to-do list down and enjoy my evening. Once I've done this review, I know my CTO Samantha is preparing for the week ahead, so I don't have to worry about it.

Prep-to-Work Practices: Get More Done in Less Time

Something good coaches do is have you come into your space with a few breaths before starting any task. It's effective because it gives you a minute to transition from doing one thing to the next. When I sit down to work, I take a moment to settle in. If I'm feeling discombobulated, even as few as three or four deep breaths in and out can help me focus more effectively.

A game-changing activity before settling into work on anything is to connect to the long-term importance of that task. We've already discovered that tasks are steps to projects. Projects are steps to bigger projects. Bigger projects are steps to your vision for your life. Your vision for your life is a step to your purpose. It's all leading to the same place: you having a great life. Just take a minute and do whatever you have to do to connect to your long-term importance. Please don't expect that the importance of a given task is going to be explicit to your CTO.

When you take a moment to connect each task you are working on to your bigger reasons for working on it, you are relating to hot goals that you have established, leading to your CTO becoming more engaged. For me, this pre-work practice is particularly important when I have to do tasks that I'm not naturally fond of but that are part of me achieving my vision and purpose of making dreams come true. One aspect of my work that I find less enjoyable is self-promotion. It would be nice if we didn't have to explain to people why we could help them, and they just knew. But why would they?

Say, for example, I pitched myself to do a talk—not my favorite thing to do, but it would allow me to impact and improve the lives of the people in the audience. This would be an ideal time to remind my CTO that the task I'm about to do is connected to my purpose and vision. When I connect to my most meaningful goals before doing a task, I can find joy in (almost) any activity.

Living Your Values

Another thing that's important to bring to your work sessions is conscious alignment with the values you've chosen to practice. The best way to do so is to have your values posted within view wherever you like to work. Take a moment to consider them and how they will be evident as you work on your task. This is a short but critical reminder. As I mentioned earlier, if your vision is your ultimate destination and your purpose is your fuel, your values are your vehicle to getting where you want to go. Stay aligned to a progressive set of values and you can expect to get anywhere faster.

Pinch-Hit Practice: Learn Anything Faster

If you are in the midst of an ongoing project, the Keep, Stop, Start tool will help you make continuous improvements to how you work. It works as it sounds. In order to do your best work today, what do you want to keep doing (what worked well)? What do you want to stop doing (such as too much time on social media), and what will you add to improve your results?

Working on this book offers a great example of the Keep, Start, Stop activity. As I pushed closer to my manuscript deadline, I felt I was running out of time. Each day, I carved out a certain number of hours to write. Invariably, my plans did not work out as I hoped. I knew I had to keep my mind positively focused, so I could keep the dopamine drip going. At the same time, I had to be real with the fact that there were some days I got far less work done than I hoped, and I was worried I wouldn't get everything done in time. It was critical for me to have a more can-do mindset or I would have failed. After all, as the expression goes, "Whether you think you can or you think you can't, you're probably right." (Thank you, Henry Ford.)

The Keep, Stop, Start Tool

Here's an example of what my Keep, Stop, Start activity might have sounded like around that time:

Keep . . . doing my Thinking Vitamins every morning; giving myself a Happygram each evening; connecting to my purpose and how my book is a part of me expressing my purpose; thinking about how I would talk to my muse (my ideal reader for the book) if I get stuck on how to explain something; leaving my phone in another room; listening to focus music; imagining myself submitting my manuscript twelve hours before the deadline.

Stop . . . being down on myself when I don't hit my word count projections; measuring success by word count; dramatizing what I haven't done and downplaying what I have accomplished; agonizing over a paragraph or sentence that's not flowing; letting the dogs in my office; keeping my phone in my office; checking social media.

Start . . . reviewing my outline plan for each chapter the night before I'm scheduled to work on it, so my brain starts to think about it; leaving the house for a coffee shop if there are too many distractions at home; creating a note for myself in the manuscript if I'm stuck on a section and moving on; getting up and stretching, exercising, meditating, or walking the dogs if I'm becoming distracted or feel stuck.

The Keep, Stop, Start activity will sound different every time you do it. The goals of this activity are to keep the dopamine flowing to your CTO for all of the things you're doing well, be practical but not dramatic about the things that aren't working, and imagine yourself introducing anything you plan to start in order to transfer the ideas over to your CTO.

If you can predict any possible obstacles to the work in front of you, you could go back to the contingency planning activity or try this Keep, Stop, Start activity to figure out how you will overcome them. When you do the Keep, Stop, Start activity this way, you are constantly grooming your CTO for what you do and don't want to continue.

The New Master of Distraction

Kids these days and their phones! Am I right? Well, it's not just them. I strongly recommend you create boundaries with your own phone. A starting place would be not to look at your phone for the first hour of your day. This is an important practice because phones, and more accurately the apps on our phones, have been designed by people who understand how dopamine works. A somewhat negative way you get dopamine is through something known as random reinforcement. Random reinforcement teaches us that unpredictability causes addictive (dopamine-producing) behavior.

People who design apps know this. To make apps addictive, designers ensure there are as many unpredictable elements as possible in your apps. Whether you go online to check your messages, check on the likes a given post received, or see whether there is anything new to look at on your feed, those things are giving you hits of dopamine, but they are stealing more from you in the process.

Every time you look at something, you're taking your attention away from something that matters, and you are letting someone else control your attention. You've probably heard this, but I'll reinforce it here anyway. There's no such thing as multitasking; all that's possible is rapid moving back and forth between tasks. And your ability to move this way is not really all that rapid. Science has shown that when you move your attention back and forth, you can lose as much as fifteen minutes each time.

Your Device and Social Media

Uninterrupted work is critical if you want to do more in less time. When you spend time on activities that have no positive benefit (I'm talking to you, funny pet video on YouTube watcher), what happens is you've stolen time that could have spent on making your dreams coming true and infused yourself with feelings of guilt or regret.

Your device is a grim reaper that threatens to steal this time from you. In order to get this book done, which I did over the Christmas holidays, I went on a social media diet. I removed all social media apps from my phone. I did not post. I did not maintain any of my platforms or write updates. I didn't send out newsletters to my community. All I did was work on my book. I'm not always this drastic, but well, I had to choose between completing my book by the deadlines I had been given or social media. It was an easy decision.

I recommend whenever you are working that you have your phone in another room. Just having it nearby and seeing the screen light up can be a distraction. For at least half of my waking day (and usually more), my phone is not with me. At the least, I want you to start out by giving yourself the first and last hour of every day away from your phone.

Getting Back on Track

From time to time, I still get off track with my time practices. When I do, my productivity starts to suffer. I recall this past summer having some of the worst productivity that I've had in a long time. I realized I wasn't using my time practices. Fortunately, I know that admonishing myself for not doing something is likely to limit my productivity even more. Instead, I reminded myself of how productive I am when I use my daily and weekly time practices, and I started using them again.

Invariably, this happens when one of my notebooks becomes full, and I don't get around to replacing it. I now buy my notebooks in bulk, so I always have a stash to maintain my system and flow. It's kind of like having coffee or ink for my printer in the cupboard. I make sure it's always there.

The World Doesn't Cooperate

Even as a specialist in this field, I have dealt with the same obstacles as you. My most recent challenge came while writing this book. I had all my notebooks, my space, my systems on my training, and everything else I needed to be productive.

Was I productive? Nope.

I spent three days struggling. It drove me crazy. It was right before Christmas, and even with my social media diet, there were so many things competing for my attention: visitors from out of town, family parties, and for some unknown reason, my partner had my puppy fixed that week, so my pup needed extra love and attention.

I was frustrated. Despite using all of my time practices, I was not achieving what I needed to. There were distractions all around me that I couldn't figure out how to escape.

One of the issues was that I use dictation as part of my writing. I couldn't just dictate in my office space, which would annoy the people around me; the same goes for a coffee shop. I needed to be somewhere quiet. One day, at the end of my rope, I decided to go to my favorite place—the beach. It was winter, but it didn't matter. I sat in my car with my hat and cut-off mittens on, a biting wind blowing off the lake, and I worked on this book.

The takeaway: don't let frustrating situations get the best of you, either. Be willing to do what it takes to succeed.

Making It Yours

The daily and weekly time practices I use match my life, and you need practices to match yours, too. With all this knowledge, you can now adapt and mold the system to create one that is a perfect fit for you. There's always a lag time between starting to use a system and using it well. You can't tell if it's going to work for you or how much benefit you'll receive unless you do it for a while. If you don't already have a way of organizing your time that you love, put this system into play for a month.

If you have been wondering whether I use online tools or old-fashioned ones, for me the handwritten system has been most effective. I have noticed when I handwrite things, my CTO is more engaged. One practical reason for this is I don't always keep my phone with me because it limits my productivity. Furthermore, when I see a notebook or journal on my table, I know it's my to-do notebook or planning journal, and it's calling to me to put something in it. In keeping my system offline, I am creating objects and symbols that speak directly to my CTO.

If you are already using Evernote or another organization system and it works for you, then go for it. Whatever you choose to do, do it. That's the number one thing that's going to ensure your success. And just calibrate, calibrate, calibrate until you find your magic formula. The idea here is not to become a slave to a process or SOP. SOPs are to serve goals; in this case, the goal is your unstoppable productivity as you work on things you will feel proud about. The priority is helping you introduce practices that enable you to get more done in less time.

Having Enough Time

Trina, a participant in Ignite, was amazed after introducing the time practices from this chapter. Before Ignite, she had struggled to find the time to work on her novel. Trina had written plays, articles, and short stories, but her dream was to complete a novel. Her book was half-written and stayed that way for years. There were all kinds of reasons—family responsibilities, not enough time, or her muse had taken a vacation. She saw these obstacles for what they were, excuses, but was at a loss about how to overcome them.

As she followed the same performance system I've been sharing with you in this book, Trina diligently did the work and, at each phase, noticed progressive improvements in how she was thinking, feeling, and approaching her writing. The chapter where she had to illuminate old and unproductive activities made a big difference. The time practices in this chapter brought Trina's transformation home.

When I checked in with Trina after the program, she sent me this lovely passage to describe her new relationship with time:

> *Don't control time. Don't try to fight it. Stop thinking time is limiting your success. Start seeing time as your partner, as a tool that allows you to achieve. There is all the time in the world to reach your goal. The time is there. It's how you use it. Free yourself of time constraints. Instead, flow with time toward your seemingly impossible goal.*

I was thrilled at what she had learned. Within months of completing the program, Trina had found her purpose, refined her goal, and completed the first draft of the novel that had eluded her for years. It was exciting to witness such fast transformation, and that's exactly what can happen to you, too. On a side note, Trina says she realized her muse was just her CTO in fancy clothes, so instead of chasing after her, they are now working together.

Whatever your leap project is and whatever active assignment you have chosen, when you add the daily, weekly, prep-to-work, and pinch-hit time practices you have learned in this chapter to the preparation and planning you have done to this point, you will raise your motivation to unimaginable levels. By using Happygrams, you will reward your CTO with dopamine to make positive connections, and like Trina, you will find yourself flowing toward what you had previously thought was a seemingly impossible goal.

Your productivity equation is nearly complete. All that's left is to teach you the tools and practices that will ensure you rise above and come out ahead, even if you face significant setbacks or (temporary) failure.

CHAPTER 11:

The Elephant in the Room

Not to brag, but I'm extremely good at failing. I am so good at failing that there was a time I was (unknowingly) rather insensitive to people who weren't. At one of my live training sessions, I shared an inspiring TED Talk. After pressing pause, I looked back at the group, ready to dive into a discussion about the vital role failure plays in winning. There was a participant who had said nothing all day; I was excited to see her shifting in her chair. Something had obviously triggered her, and I assumed it was an epiphany about the value of failure. I called on her and asked her what her "aha" moment was.

I wasn't prepared for her reply.

She blurted out, "This goes against everything I have learned my whole life. School never wanted me to fail. Teachers never celebrated me when I failed. My parents never celebrated me when my report card wasn't good enough. My bosses didn't cheer for me when I failed. When I share my failure with people who are closest to me, they're not all excited that I am closer to success. They're worried about me. I just don't get this."

That was my wake-up call. I was the one who had an epiphany that day. I realized she was right, and she wasn't alone in thinking the way she did. There's all this talk about the value of failure, but we don't truly embrace it when our friends, family members, colleagues, and neighbors fail. It was the elephant in the room.

Do you cheer for your child's terrible report card and think to yourself that you have the next Steve Jobs or Lori Greiner on your hands? Or do you worry about their future? Did your client give you a big, fat bonus the last time your work was below par because they saw it as a sure sign you were on to bigger and better things? Do you automatically think "winner" when you see someone fall short of a big goal, or do you think they're taking on too many risks? If someone you know has been trying something for five or even ten years, is the cultural norm for everyone around that person to say, "Cool, you're one step closer to your solution?"

I realized that if Thomas Edison—who, according to legend, found 999 ways not to create a lightbulb before succeeding—was working in a university today, his peers might be more inclined to wonder how his lab continued to obtain funding than believe he was on the precipice of success.

Getting Real about Failure

Our dialogue and behavior around failing do not match up. How do we distinguish failures that result because we didn't apply ourselves correctly from those that occur because we took an educated risk that didn't work out? How do we get our CTO on board with failure when it is programmed to protect us from harm? We need to have a more in-depth conversation—not one that simply celebrates failure as a path to success, which it can be, but a conversation that gets real about how to truly make failure a path to success, which is something few people achieve.

The idea that failure is a path to success in business is well celebrated but typically after the fact. Once success has been achieved, it is easy to see how certain failures guided a person on their road to achievement. It's much harder to see failure as the teacher it could be when it's standing right in front of you, feeling like an obstacle or setback. Unfortunately, the process for how to win from failure is not well-known. This disconnect is causing unnecessary suffering, confusion, and sadness, leaving people who are facing failure without a lifeline, hanging onto the hope that failure will lead to winning but without a process to ensure it will.

If you are someone who fully embraces failure when it comes your way, congratulations. That's wonderful. Despite failure's popularity as a strategy for success, your response is rare, and you should be proud of your ability to handle adversity so well. You can skip this chapter. For the rest of us, failure can lead to embarrassment and shame. We're frightened our plans may never work out and apprehensive about moving forward because our past decisions didn't work out. If you don't know what steps to take to transform your failures into shortcuts to your dreams, this is the chapter for you.

Why We Need a New Dialogue

I think everybody has an idea of what it means to fail, as well as different tolerance levels for failure. What feels like a bump in the road to one person can feel like a grenade going off to another. Running a restaurant is a great way to develop the reflex to turn grenades into bumps. I faced bad news almost daily. Once, I discovered a large tax I didn't know I needed to pay the government. There was the time the landlord opened a "massage parlor" over our classy neighborhood restaurant. Staff would call in sick at the last minute. Clients would book tables and not show up. Suppliers would short-ship us or send us bills for things we didn't order. The restaurant business is high stress because, by definition, people are showing up at their grumpiest—when they're hungry.

For the first few years, there were days when things got so bad I didn't think I could take it anymore. But, over time, I developed the ability to turn sour situations into sweet ones. Those years of struggles and setbacks taught me skills I was previously lacking. My clients often remark on my ability to find possibilities in the midst of adversity. I'm sure this comes from my restaurant days. My regular experience handling stressful situations programmed my CTO to accept that when we hit a bump in the road, the wheels don't fall off. We just keep going. Of course, not everyone has had this kind of conditioning—the student at my live training session certainly hadn't—so there's a need to teach the skills and thought processes that enable you to turn frustrating situations into remarkable ones.

Lag Time versus Failure

Lag time is something everybody experiences when they make a change. We all know that to get new results, we need to do new things. But when we try new things, the results aren't always as quick as we'd like them to be.

My mother is a gardener, and if she put a seed in a seed tray and nurtured it for a week and didn't get a sprout, she wouldn't throw it out. She would continue to nurture that little seed in its tray, understanding it's going to take more than a week to start seeing progress. I think many people forget lag time is to be expected between taking action and seeing results. We make changes to what we're doing; we try new ideas for two or three weeks, perhaps a couple of months, and when we don't see fully-bloomed plants in front of us, we're frustrated, give up, and decide it wasn't the right seed—or, in this case, the right idea. We go hunting for a new one.

Let's say, if there was a failure scale, lag time is a one out of ten. You're doing the right things, but you haven't done them long enough to see results. I think many people who work on their own suffer from the lag time effect. They're so impatient for their businesses to work that when something doesn't produce immediate results, they want to give up. We compare ourselves to others and their businesses. We think other people are getting all these amazing results, and we're not. But the problem is that we just didn't give that idea enough time to take root.

Ask any overnight success their backstory, and they'll tell you about years of trial and error and struggles to reach the top. In Basecamp, we help clients establish signature programs so they can create predictable revenue. Even with us by their side, ensuring they follow the most efficient process, it takes most people a year or more to execute all the projects in the exploration phase. When it comes to lag time, the failure might be pulling the plug too early, not the idea itself.

Embracing Iteration

The TED Talk I mentioned at the start of the chapter is Tom Wujec's talk, "Build a Tower, Build a Team." In it, Wujec illustrates the value of keeping your eye on a singular destination and adjusting your course until you get there (and why kindergarteners outperform MBA students at a simple creative task). Wujec has a humorous way of illustrating the formula for achieving something new: You have to know where you are, where you want to go, and fill in the gap.

I've enjoyed boating since I was a child. We'd often set out on Lake Temagami in northern Ontario for the long boat ride to our cottage. One of the islands on the way was called Three Tree Island. We needed to head for Three Tree Island because if we didn't, we could end up on the rocks. Three Tree Island is about the size of a Starbucks bathroom, so it isn't a very big target. On the way, there were always wind, waves, and other boats to contend with, each taking us off course a few degrees here, a few degrees there, so we were continually correcting our course to stay on our route to Three Tree Island. There was no throwing in the towel. We had to keep pointing at that island, or we'd end up on the rocks.

Achieving business goals is like a boat ride to the cottage. We start with a destination in mind, we're pointing toward our vision—arriving at our cottage—and working on our subgoal, reaching Three Tree Island, so we don't end up on the rocks. Along the way, wind and waves buffet us. Storms might roll in. Do we quit if the lake gets rough, and we're taken off course? If we weren't out in the middle of a lake, we might be able to switch boats. But the boat—the business idea we've committed to—isn't the problem. Any boat is going to get taken off course on its way to Three Tree Island.

If you've chosen a leap project that's linked to your purpose, puts you on course for your pathfinder vision, and is at the appropriate stage of the Knowledge Business Growth Model, then your goal is not the problem.

Reaching it has everything to do with your ability to adjust course when the weather changes. The weather always changes. Every business owner has to navigate around obstacles and adapt to changes outside their control. It's better to prepare for the challenges than pretend your path to success will be the exception.

Setting your sights on a target and quitting before you reach it sets you back every time. Think of the farming industry. Where would we be if every time there was a drought, a pest infestation, or an early frost, all the farmers gave up and plowed over their fields? We'd be in trouble. But thankfully, they've learned to plan and weather those storms. You will have to do the same if you want to build a business that is easier to manage than your way of doing business now.

What Happens When We Hide

For a culture that seeks happiness, we go about it all wrong. We think the way to get there is to paint smiles on our faces when things hurt and to fake feeling okay when we aren't. This is where the idea, "What you resist persists," comes into play. It is absolutely the case that if you try to hide from what happened or not face up to it, it is going to turn it into something bigger. Ignore that puddle from the leak in a roof, and soon you'll have a flood.

Have you ever had a problem with someone, decided not to talk to them about it, and then magically, your relationship with that person started getting better and better and closer and closer? Or did it go the other way? The same dynamic goes on between you and your CTO. If you're hurt, and you try to bury that hurt and pretend it isn't there, you'll move further away from healing. Your hurts won't stay hidden; they will program instructions to your CTO, and you will find similar stories playing out over and over again.

What we need to do when we're distraught about a situation is to accept what happened. Become curious. "Oh, that's interesting," we might say. "This situation is upsetting me. There must be a lesson in here somewhere, but right now I feel worried, and I'm going to honor that. I'm going to sit with that. I'm going to pay attention to my body and notice where I feel discomfort. And when I find the location of my discomfort, maybe it's in my throat or the pit of my stomach or my temples, I'm just going to breathe into it gently and allow it to be there. I know discomfort is a sign there's an opportunity for me to discover and reprogram a hot goal, but reprogramming my CTO can wait. My first step is just neutrally accepting that I feel like crap right now."

Grief Is Neurochemical

There was a time when I worked on a tech startup about death. It was going to be focused on helping people support someone bereaved. I worked on that project for over a year, and it didn't go anywhere because our team couldn't get it together. But in the process, I learned a lot about grief and how it affects people and how to support people when they are grieving.

I learned we have a set of neurochemicals that affect how we feel. Sometimes when someone is hurting, we try to talk them out of it. We encourage them to smile, to shake it off. Or, unhelpfully, we offer, "Well, just think; there are a lot of people who are far worse off than you."

But people who are experiencing grief are also producing neurochemicals that are causing them to feel the way they are feeling. Like cortisol, which is our primary stress hormone and can stay in the body for twenty-four to forty-eight hours once triggered. Once grief neurochemicals are triggered, their effects are physically running their course in our bodies as well.

You can't smile your way around neurochemistry. Telling someone or yourself to stop feeling upset doesn't help. That is equivalent to telling someone who has had too much to drink to stop being intoxicated. The body has to process and rid itself of the alcohol to end the intoxication, and that takes time. When we fail, we feel alone and isolated. We experience stress. Cortisol is released. In the same way, neurochemicals have to be processed out of the body to relieve the feelings. Turning failures into wins is important, but first, you must address what's going on physiologically.

Practice to Overcome Failure

What do you do when you out-and-out miss Three Tree Island and end up on the rocks? Here are some tools that will get you back into the game. If you learn to use these tools, you will eventually start rebounding automatically. There is an old seventies ballad, "The First Cut is the Deepest," and it's true. It might feel impossible now, but if you keep doing this, eventually you will turn those grenades into bumps. In this section, I will share multiple techniques you can follow to overcome situations you feel have overwhelmed you.

There is an analogy I like to use with helicopters and hummingbirds. You are a helicopter when you get up and survey a situation from above and a hummingbird when you get busy, task-focused, and down to work. Invariably, events that feel like failures happen when you've been in hummingbird mode, focused on your tasks, and something stops you in your tracks. A problem. A catastrophe. The first thing to do is to determine what has happened and figure out why. Get into helicopter mode, and being as neutral as possible, take a good look at the landscape to evaluate what has taken place.

Release Resistance

The easiest way for me to teach you how to release resistance is for you to do an activity. It's going to feel uncomfortable at first, but if you are brave enough to give it a try, you'll experience something remarkable.
I want you to go ahead and read through the instructions below, and when you are done, come back to this point and do this activity with your eyes closed.

Think of something that makes you uncomfortably fearful. You don't need to think of the most frightening thing you've ever encountered. A snake or spider will do if that works for you. For me, it's worms. Those things are so creepy. Think of something that makes you feel uncomfortably fearful enough to try this activity.

Once you've settled on something, I want you to do the opposite of what everybody else has probably told you to do in the past when you feel fear: I want you to stay with it. That's correct. Don't try to feel better. Allow yourself to experience whatever it is that you're feeling.

One of the things we have been taught is to fear what makes us uncomfortable. But this just keeps us small. So much fear is in our minds. Think about it. Where are you right now? Somewhere where you can read this book. Whatever upset you are feeling is in your mind. It's your CTO who is afraid. It's worried that something will hurt you even though you are not in imminent danger.

I want you to stay with whatever you are feeling. If you can, try to locate in your body where you feel uncomfortable or restricted. If you can find that spot, breathe into it. Breathe deeply, gently, and quietly, and stay with whatever you're feeling. Breathe in and out as you stay with your feeling of discomfort.

Continue thinking about the fearful thing you chose as you breathe into it. Don't try to close your mind to it. Don't try to think of something pleasant. Just notice what's happening in your body. Notice your physical sensations. Just sit with the emotions. If you still have the fear, and it's still feeling strong, stay with it and keep breathing into it.

You'll feel when it's time to open your eyes because your feeling of stress will start to ease. Sit with the activity until your discomfort dissipates.

Now, return to the beginning of these instructions, and do this activity. When you are finished, continue to the next section for the debriefing.

Releasing Resistance Activity Debrief

When I do this activity in my group programs, my program participants are always amazed. I can see how doubtful they are of me when we begin. There's sweat on some of their brows (on video cameras) as they do the activity. But what happens at the end? Surprising calm. The boogie monster did not come and eat them. They felt something fearfully upsetting. They breathed into it. They stayed with it. And then at some magical moment, their CTO realized they were okay. They weren't under threat. It simmered down. And everything was fine.

Perhaps when you first started the activity, your chest, jaw, or neck was tight. You could feel your heart rate increase, or maybe your gut clenched. Maybe you were apprehensive and scared, but as you kept breathing calmly, your fear lessened. Why is that? When you first start imagining things, your CTO can't tell the difference between something that is imagined and something real. When you think of something that you have a habitual fear response to, your CTO is doing its job.

But as you breathe into what you feel, your CTO comes to realize that you're safe, your environment is secure, and there is nothing to worry about. And this is how you can release fear. No amount of running from fear will ever help you release it because when you run from something, you are telling your CTO that it's dangerous, and you're afraid of it. You are reinforcing the dread and anxiety.

Acceptance Equals Release

We've been taught to cheer ourselves up the second we get down. But that's not the way to permanently release pain. I learned about this during my extensive rehabilitation after my car accident. It's okay to feel uncomfortable, but resistance tells your CTO there's something to be scared of. That's why resistance makes things stronger.

Feelings you don't like don't go away through resisting them. People say to breathe, but you also want to turn inward and face the fear inside your body. What did you experience when you went inside, felt the fear, found it, and breathed into it? Did you experience what my group participants do? Did you release your fear? (I still don't like worms, but I don't resist them the way I used to.)

Positive psychology gives us another way to release fear. Label what you are experiencing: "I'm feeling fearful and stressed and embarrassed and ashamed." Breathe into it and talk to your CTO with love. "I'm okay. It's okay. We're going to get through this together. We're going to be okay. We're going to be safe." Label it, and breathe into it. When your CTO hears your calm, relaxed tone of voice, it will know there is nothing to be afraid of.

A vital pointer: Notice that you say, "I am *feeling* fearful and stressed," not "I *am* fearful and stressed" (or whatever feeling you are experiencing). It's important not to confuse labeling yourself and labeling your emotions. Your emotions are temporary reactions to the meaning you assign events that have taken place. They are states of being you can control by changing how you view what has taken place.

Depending on how much an event wipes you out, the process may take you more or less time to release resistance.

What Revives You?

Once you have released resistance, it is time to turn your attention to feeling better. To help speed up regeneration, think of who or what inspires you. Do you have books that inspire you? Can you think of TED Talks that make you feel invincible? Is there a TV show or movie that brings you back? What about music? Perhaps it's a place in nature where you like to go or a pet who comforts you. Are you lucky enough to have a person in your life who can always make you feel better? Whatever your solution is, do it.

If I'm down, one of my favorite pick-me-ups is to listen to the Eminem song "Lose Yourself." I first heard it in his movie *8 Mile,* which I found so inspirational. When I listen to his song, it brings me right back to the movie. I think of all the hard times he went through, and then I think to myself, "Come on, Jill, get up."

The best time to think about your pick-me-ups is before you need one. Pretend you are in *The Sound of Music,* and make a list of your favorite things. For me, that list includes walks on the beach with my dogs, Quinte and Rocket, visits with my nephew, or watching a comedy or action film. I also have a few inspired friends who know just what to say to pick me up on my darkest days.

Take a moment and make a list for yourself right now; it's good to make a pick-me-up list when you're feeling strong because you'll always know it's there. Any time you come across something that makes you feel incurably awesome, add it to your list. When you have bad days, you'll

188 IT'S GO TIME

remember your list and put it into action. That's the personalized first-aid kit that will pick you up when life knocks you down.

Recovery Procedure for Failure

Once you've gotten over the initial upset from an event that felt like a failure to you, you've released your resistance and done a few activities to make yourself feel better. Continue with the next steps to convert your failure into a lesson you won't repeat. The five steps to turn a failure into a lesson are:

1. Evaluate what happened.
2. Take 100 percent responsibility.
3. Forgive yourself.
4. Apply *amor fati*.
5. Regroup, code a contingency, move on.

Evaluate What Happened

Whenever you face a situation you perceive as a failure, when you first look at it, you're almost certainly seeing it for worse than it is. Start by getting a clear picture of what took place by listing the sequence of events. Focus on facts, tangible things that happened, and exclude any opinions.

To do this, you will include things like dates, times, and exact words people spoke. Do not allow yourself to add any stories or meanings.

It is critical to avoid assigning any meaning to what happened—good or bad—and to simply gather and examine the facts as if you were a judge presiding over a court of law or an investigator interviewing a crime suspect.

Take 100 Percent Responsibility

Something essential to let go of is resentment and blame. It's not possible to go through this life without crossing paths with people who disappoint or hurt us. What we need to remember is that it's not just us being run by our CTOs; everybody is.

Consider my client Richard's story in Chapter 3. A large company had offered to fund his tech start-up and then backed out. When I first started working with Richard, it was his instinct to be upset with the company for using its power to leave him in a lurch. He felt he would never have taken a second mortgage on his home if he'd sensed any possibility of duplicitous behavior on their part.

I felt for Richard, but I knew his best way back to being in charge of his life was to take responsibility for his role in what had happened. No one forced him to take the second mortgage. Richard chose to take that risk, and the best thing he could do with that information was to gain self-awareness of his tolerance for risk.

As much as the other company behaved poorly, if Richard continued to blame them, he would never get back in the driver's seat of his life. Richard chose not to sue the company because there was little chance he would prevail against their high-priced lawyers. It was an unfortunate situation, but if Richard didn't take one hundred percent responsibility for taking out the mortgage and choosing not to sue, then he wouldn't be in a position to regain control of his life.

I know how counterintuitive that can feel, but the problem with holding onto resentment is that as long as you do, you won't have control of your life. The pain you are carrying will program your CTO in ways that will keep you from the success you want in your future. As long as you insist on hanging on to that pain, your CTO will be getting inadvertent programming cues to set hot goals, which will perpetually increase your unhappiness.

Richard came to understand this. Once he took responsibility for the situation, he felt lighter and more empowered about his future than when he was laying blame on others for what happened.

When you forgive someone, you are not saying what they did was okay. You are acknowledging that they (and their CTO) did the best they could or that they didn't know any better. More importantly, you are making a choice to be in the driver's seat of your life. And you will need to be in that seat to achieve the success you want.

Forgive Yourself

What would it be like if you could forgive yourself for all your perceived wrongdoings? I think it's a shame how hard we are on ourselves. We take on challenging goals that we've never been trained to achieve, we do our best to prepare ourselves, bootstrap, make the best of situations, and sometimes we falter. How on earth are we supposed to be good at everything? Never mind that most of our actions are dictated by a CTO who has been programmed since our childhood.

I invite you to consider that you have never done anything wrong, that you have always done your best, given your circumstances and the conditioning of your CTO.

No matter what blame you have laid on yourself, as you did with releasing blame of others, let it go. When you want to be in control of your present you need to let go of and forgive yourself for all perceived failures from your past. The sooner you can bring yourself to forgive yourself, the faster you will heal and move forward with a life you want.

Apply *Amor Fati*

Reframing is a big part of bringing the *amor fati* value to life. As a reminder, *amor fati* means to love fate, and the idea is to force yourself to find a way to turn situations to your advantage.

Have you ever thought an event was the worst thing that could possibly have happened when it first occurred and then, in retrospect, looked back and realized it was the best thing that could have happened? Take Dr. Spencer Silver's case. He worked at 3M and was tasked with producing a super-strong adhesive. He failed. His glue ended up weak. Instead of throwing it away and starting over, he found another use for his "failed adhesive," and Post-it notes were born.

Whether you see an event as good or bad has everything to do with your beliefs, which are a form of hot goals. We are wired to perceive the goings-on in life through the filters of the programming from our past. We lose a client, but then we discover they would have been exhausting to work with, and a better client comes along. We don't get a job, but then we build our ideal business. Or, in my case, if I hadn't been hit by a car, I might have ended up living a life not nearly as fulfilling as the one I have created for myself now.

We have the power to reframe everything about our lives. Sometimes, when I start working with people, they are focused on all the things they don't have. Then we look at a list of their assets, and they realize they have supportive friends, marketable skills, a roof over their heads, and people around them who would help them in a time of need.

I encourage you to look at any lousy situation you've experienced, and consider how it could turn out to be the best thing that could have happened to you.

Regroup, Code a Contingency, Move On

Your current location is always changing. If you get stuck or lose focus, come back to this book, regroup, and figure out what's missing. Start with Phase I, figuring out your current coordinates. Where you are is always in flux. Reconnect with your purpose, which is probably a sapling at this point. Consider whether you're still working in alignment with your vision for what you want three years from now. Explore whether you are living up to the values you identified as being most important to you. Is anything out of alignment? If yes, calibrate.

Once you've done that, move on to Phase II, checking in with your leap project and active assignment. Are you working on the best possible project, or did you get sidetracked and start focusing on something else? Or, perhaps you feel aimless because you completed the project you were working on, and it's time to choose a new one?

Next, revisit the plans you created in Phase III. Are there positive signs littered all over your environment that are reminding you of the important goals you are working toward? Do a social scan. Why are you hitting roadblocks? Have you surrounded yourself with people who can help you rise to a new level of success?

If you can figure out a way to turn the situation into the best thing that ever happened to you, do it. If you can use the idea to be bigger rather than smaller than the situation, do it. If you can see no way past it, let it go. To make sure you don't make a related or similar mistake again, revisit the contingency planning activity in Chapter 9. After all, what has just happened is now a predictable obstacle. And now that it has become predictable, situations like the one you just faced become ones you know how to avoid (or, at least, they've become much easier to overcome).

Finally, move on to Phase IV. Have you been doing your Thinking Vitamins every morning? Increase the dosage to two or three times a day. And if they're not posted on your mirror anymore, get them back up there! The daily to-do lists, nightly happygrams, weekly reviews, and the keep, stop, start activities all work in harmony to help you stay on track to what you care about most.

A High-Profile Training

I had a corporate training session that went wrong. It was the worst I've ever had in my entire career. And what happened? I was fired.

It was a seminar for a management team that was new to intensive professional development. The team was in seminars from Monday to Friday, full days complete with assignments at lunch and in the evenings. For them, it was like drinking from a fire hose for a week. I was scheduled with the group on a Friday at 1:00 p.m., after a lunch where they were served pasta.

If you've never done training before, it may not be evident why this setup was a problem. The bottom line: by Friday afternoon their heads were jammed with a week's worth of new knowledge. At this point, their minds were tuned to getting home, planning for the weekend, and, thanks to a carb-heavy lunch, they were sluggish and sleepy. I knew all this, and what's worse, despite raising my concerns with the organizer, I agreed to teach them some of the most complex material I have.

The only reason you're not hearing a blizzard of adjectives right now to describe how I felt about this is that I wouldn't be taking complete responsibility if I did. Why should I take full responsibility for being placed after lunch, at the end of a week, and after a pasta lunch? I didn't choose the menu!

The truth is when I arranged that session, I suspected they were asking for the wrong material. When I first heard about the opportunity, I was asked for a session called situational leadership. It's a session that makes sense for C-suite executives who are facing complex situations. The seminar had been organized for VP and director-level managers, and I sensed the situational leadership session wasn't what they needed most.

When I suggested this to the organizer, I offered to teach a more appropriate seminar for the participants. I didn't make my case well enough, and at the slightest indication from the organizer that the client wouldn't want to change topics, I acquiesced. Why? Because the training was for a high-profile organization, and I wanted the prestige of having them as a client.

I'm sharing this story so you can see that I didn't let this experience derail me. Instead, I did the next thing on the failure recovery list. I forgave myself. "Jill, you got excited to deliver a seminar for a high-profile organization." I now know I will not do that again. I won't agree to teach content I know isn't right for the participants. I won't accept an after-lunch slot on a Friday if the group has been in training all week, and I've never met them before.

Now that I've reflected on what's happened, I will get my CTO, Samantha, on board with a quick contingency visualization, "Hey Samantha, in the future, when and if this thing happens, we will . . ." For example, "In the future, when I catch myself thinking, 'Shiny object, impressive client,' I will not accept the wrong job again. Going forward, I will watch out for similar themes, not letting the shiny prize at the end interfere with a logical assessment of the project."

That's it, folks. Don't make a big deal about failure or use it as an excuse to feel sorry for yourself. Learn from it, move on, and do what I do: cry a bit and then push through those things. Allow yourself to grieve and be sad or angry about it; otherwise, you're burying it. Then follow the steps in this section, and move on!

Don't Plan for Failure; Don't Be Afraid of It Either

Failure is not a brick wall that springs up in front of you, leaving you with no option but to turn back and try again or, worse, sit cross-legged, head in hands, and give up. Failure is a challenge. Here's the wall; now what? Well, you can grab a ladder and go over. Use a shovel to dig under it. Take a jackhammer to it. Blast a hole through it. Or, the solution could be as simple as taking a few steps sideways and walking the other way.

When you talk to successful people about their journeys, the stories they invariably love to tell are the times they fell the hardest because it makes the success feel that much sweeter. Stephen King proudly shares how his novel *Carrie* was rejected thirty times before finding a publisher. The time to face your possible failures is now, before they happen. Let your CTO know when you come to that unexpected obstacle that it's just a bump in the road on your journey to realizing your goal.

CHAPTER 12:

Your Time to Climb

When my mother was growing up, she spent her summers at her family's camp on Mount Riga in Connecticut. There were two lakes on the mountain; their depths controlled by a dam that could be used to release water into a brook that ran into the valley below. The dam's controls were located in a small building, the Dam House. The only structure on the shoreline, it was situated directly above the deepest and fastest-moving water on what was called the Upper Lake.

A rite of passage required to gain acceptance from the "cool kids" living on the mountain was jumping off the Dam House roof into the fast-flowing water below. At ten years of age, my mother was stuck in the middle—four or five years younger than the cool kids who could easily make the leap and four or five years older than a far less cool group of post-war babies.

My mother couldn't bear to spend another summer without fitting in anywhere. Although younger than the kids who could make the jump,

195

she was a strong swimmer, and she was determined to gain acceptance from their group. Her first couple of attempts fell through, but her goal was too important to give up on. She developed the mantra, "Close your eyes, hold your nose, and jump off the Dam House roof!" Sure enough, she made the jump and earned her long-desired spot among the cool kids.

Like my mother, whose rite of passage required her to jump from a roof into turbulent waters to get what she wanted, you can expect moments of truth on your journey getting from where you are now to building a business you love running and that leaves room for life. In Chapter 9, you programmed your CTO with contingencies for the obstacles you expect to arise based on your prior experiences. In this chapter, I will alert you to the top four stumbling blocks experienced by my clients and program participants as they implement the all-in system and explain how you can overcome them. The top four are:

- Not committing to a niche
- Finding stubborn hot goals
- Adopting the performance equation
- Underestimating social

Not Committing to a Niche

If you're at the point in your business where you've found what you love doing but are finding it stressful either because you're working too much or aren't attracting a steady stream of clients, then follow the Expertise Business Growth Model and start by committing to a single niche and creating a signature program for that niche.

It breaks my heart when people flounder for years because they believe they will lose business if they target only one niche. A friend and photographer, Joseph, made this mistake. Joseph creates some of the most striking and soulful lifestyle photography I have ever seen. Joseph came to me for advice after losing most of what he had after his wife left him. At the time, he was only getting occasional work shooting weddings, which given his situation, depressed him. I urged him to create a signature program or experience around his lifestyle photography in favor of the traditional photographers' model, which is to have an exhibit. He ignored my advice.

Putting on an exhibit is time-consuming, expensive, and affords negligible leverage. The photographer has to create multiple works, find a location, frame the art, and sometimes even pay for food and beverages. It's inherently inefficient because it's all or nothing on that day (week or month). Even in the best case, should a number of works sell, it's a temporary windfall that gets quickly absorbed by debt incurred to mount the show or to cover expenses in the months ahead. Unless you're a photographer with an in-demand following, pinning your hopes on an exhibit is a high-risk, low-reward endeavor.

My predictions for Joseph's art exhibit were accurate. While he felt proud about pulling the whole thing off without a hitch, he didn't generate the sales he hoped for, nor did he gain any recurring benefit from the time he invested.

Finding a Niche You Love

If Joseph had been able to see beyond the blinders of his industry's norms, he would have committed to a niche and a signature program. In Joseph's case, he might have created a signature portrait experience or a signature teaching and coaching program to teach novice photographers his secrets . . . or both if he could choose a niche that wanted both those things.

To create a business that's a joy to run, you're going to need to get clear on your target market and what problem you solve for them. When thinking of yours, I encourage you to follow the lead of my brother, Owen. His program, The Quizzical Chef, is for home cooks who are bored in the kitchen and want to make healthy and delicious meals their family will love. It's a targeted niche since he focuses on parents who want to make healthier meals their kids will want to eat!

Owen found his niche by considering his Happiness Recipe and answering two simple questions: what do I love to do, and who do I love to serve? His answers to the first question were "playing in the kitchen" and "teaching." His answer to the second question was, "curious cooks."

To find your niche, hold fast to your Happiness Recipe, and then answer those same two questions.

Finding Stubborn Hot Goals

The second stumbling block you can expect to encounter is the presence of extremely well-hidden hot goals. I called these insidious hot goals because they're sneaky. They present themselves to you as truths about your world but are, in fact, self-imposed limitations holding you back.

When it comes to how happy you are with your life, it's important to remember that your CTO is content with the life you have now. Anything you feel you do not have enough of, deep down, you actually do feel you have enough of. It's a challenging concept because it feels at odds with your emotions. But whenever you feel stuck in a frustrating pattern, the wise move is to recognize that you likely have one or more hidden hot goals that need to be discovered and reprogrammed.

In the years since I have started programming hot goals as part of my performance equation, I have made phenomenal upgrades to my business and life by crushing projects I choose in record time. Despite a long list of successes, one project I could not seem to crush with my system was writing this book. On my first attempt, I did not anticipate any problems. I used the system in this book and crafted my plan to write the book by setting aside two days each week. About a year into this plan, I ended up with sixty thousand words that I wouldn't show anyone.

On my second attempt, I decided my two-days-a-week approach wasn't immersive enough, so I put a freeze on offering my online group programs, dramatically limited my time with private clients, and booked trips to Bali (after some client work in Singapore) and Puerto Rico (to see my mom) where I could chill by the beach and write. I had a lovely time that year, but four months of chilling, swimming, and fun in the sun didn't yield anything more usable than my first attempt.

At this point, it had been a year and a half since I had become serious about writing this book, and even though my CTO, Samantha, was giving me all the signs that my conscious and subconscious goals were aligned, I knew I had an insidious hot goal because if I didn't, I would have had a book.

Investigating My Insidious Hot Goal

I donned my investigator's monocle to solve my mystery. First, I considered whether or not the hot goal was related to my discomfort around grammar, spelling, and writing because I am dyslexic. Although this seemed like it could fit, I had written a fair bit by this point in my career. I had written articles and blogs. I had written procedural manuals and training manuals. I had written well over a book to earn my master's degree! No, there was a time that might have limited me, but I was beyond that.

Next, I examined whether my insidious hot goal had to do with me being afraid of bad reviews. Again, I consider this unlikely. Although I stayed out of the limelight for years after my teacher humiliated me in front of my class in grade two, teaching online had thickened my skin when it came to receiving critical reviews. It's impossible to put ideas online that everybody is going to agree with. I'd learned a long time ago to measure my success by the people I help, not by the people who criticize me. I've received enough letters of gratitude about transformed lives to know that my work needs to get out there. Again, this was not the problem.

At this point, I was beside myself with frustration. How could this be eluding me? I am the rapid implementer! Finally, I arrived at a hypothesis that seemed to have merit. Back in that fateful grade two class when my teacher ridiculed me in front of my classmates for being dyslexic, she also told my two best friends to stop being friends with me because I would hold them back.

It occurred to me that back in grade two, I might have created a hot goal not to hold others back with my friendship. Don't get me wrong; my relationships weren't bad, but I did often feel awkward around others— out of place. It struck me that when you write a book focused on teaching, you don't write it for a niche or target audience. You write it for one person, a muse who is your source of inspiration, and you tell that person what you want them to know. It requires deep authenticity.

200 | IT'S GO TIME

The Breakthrough Clue

I got excited. Consciously, I knew I had a positive impact on others and that if I still had a hot goal from my grade two class, I could certainly reprogram it. I signed up for a course that taught how about to be more authentic in relationships. Initially, I had a negative reaction to the course. Despite it being held in a neighborhood I was familiar with, I made three wrong turns on my way there. It was rush hour, and I was annoyed. I sensed my CTO, Samantha, was trying to keep me from that course. It didn't feel safe.

I forced myself to get to the course because I've learned to lean into situations that I strongly resist. Remember, what you resist, persists. Within a matter of weeks—though after a good deal more resistance and many tears—I experienced a breakthrough in my relationships across the board. I felt more comfortable being myself. I was more authentic and became closer with my family and friends. Critically, I had finally identified and reprogrammed the insidious hot goal that had been keeping me from writing this book. The relationship course was in September. Four months later, I had completed my manuscript.

As you work with this system, expect to crush some projects more easily than others. Be prepared for some of your hot goals to be less obvious, more difficult to find, and harder to reprogram. If you have something that, like my book, has eluded you, even though you've used all the tools in this book, take heart. All is not lost. Remind yourself that every single hot goal you have can be reprogrammed by a sudden emotional experience, decision, or vow, or through repetition.

If you're stumped, ask an intuitive friend to work through the material in this book with you. And I invite you to visit www.boomu.com to learn more about our programs Ignite: Activate Your Big Idea and Basecamp: Increase Your Impact with a Signature Program. Over the years, we've learned how to speed up the process of helping people discover and reprogram their limiting hot goals.

Adopting the Performance Equation

My clients and program participants often resist the number of steps involved in the performance equation I've taught you in this book. After all, every time you come up with a new project, active assignment, subgoal, or sub-subgoal, you have to develop a goal statement using the MOMA Method and create a big picture staircase strategy and a nitty-gritty plan. It's a *lot* of work!

When I'm teaching this material live, there is always someone who will ask, "Must we really do it all? If we can only do one part of it, what should we do?" If you've wondered the same thing, I'll tell you what I tell them. Take on fewer projects so you can use the complete performance equation every time. A key differentiator between high-performance experts and everybody else is that high-performance experts know the fewer projects they take on and commit to, the more successful they will be.

Do you know the fable "The Three Little Pigs?" On the remote chance you don't, in the story, three little pigs each build a house—the first from straw, the second from sticks, and the third from bricks. Along comes a big bad wolf who loves to eat little pigs. He lays the first two houses to waste with a couple of targeted huffs and puffs, and the pigs run for their lives to their brother's brick house. The wolf's luck changes, however, when he tries to blow down the brick house. The wolf fails when he climbs down the chimney instead and meets his demise in a fire the third little pig set to greet him.

Timeless Advice from a Fable

Although I find "The Three Little Pigs" an odd story to share with small children before bed, I encourage you to take a page from the third little pig's playbook when it comes to the performance equation. A bonus? Using the performance equation takes much less time and effort than building a brick house! With a little practice, you'll discover that it only takes ten to thirty minutes of planning to set yourself up to achieve more in everything you do. I ask, why would you take on a project that you would spend days, weeks, months, or even years to achieve, and not be willing to spend a few minutes on setting yourself up for more success?

Even a project as simple as getting testimonials benefits from developing a MOMA goal. For example, when most people want testimonials they simply ask people for a testimonials and often get testimonials that are not all that helpful. Did you know that for a testimonial to be helpful it must demonstrate the before and after results your clients got with you?

Our MOMA goal statement for obtaining testimonials for our programs is to illustrate our participants' transformations in a way that helps people considering our programs see themselves in our participants' stories. Our success metrics are:

- Our personality/what it's like to do take a program with us shines through
- The testimonials express outcomes reflective of those we promise on signup
- Applicants tell us they applied because they saw themselves in a testimonial!

If you would like to see some of our testimonials you can check them out at www.boom-u.com.

If you've had the urge to try to cherry-pick this performance system, try the following. For the next month, use chapters 7-9 to plan every project, big and small. Whether you're developing your signature program, writing a book, planning a blog, hiring a freelancer, or creating a website, use it. If you do, I am confident you will see how much more you accomplish and how the process quickens as you gain experience with it. Your reward will be the foundations of a business that even a big bad wolf won't be able to blow down.

Underestimating Social

A number of my clients have attempted to upgrade their businesses and lives with the all-in system and hope for change while maintaining their current social circumstances. They continue to spend time with the same people, don't add new people, and wonder why they are not making progress. I call having goals for change while maintaining your social circumstances trying to outsmart the power of social, and I have never seen it work.

Science has shown time and again that we become an average of the people we spend time around. If there is anything about your life or business that you are not happy with, you can be sure that your social circumstances are the number one contributing factor. As I explained earlier in the book, you are always setting hot goals, whether you are intentionally trying to create them or not. I also explained how your CTO instinctively creates prevention hot goals—hot goals that keep you safe.

Historically, being part of a social group has been essential for our survival. Your CTO instinctively acclimatizes to the people you spend time with because doing so protects your social network and helps keep you safe. People like people who are like them. The more similar you are to the people in a group, the more likely they are to welcome you. We can't outsmart our human instinct to acclimatize to our social group; it's all happening subconsciously.

When to Prioritize Social

When you are happy with your business and life, you won't need to adjust your social. When you are not, getting yourself into a social network that matches what you want should be one of your top priorities. The relationships that will support you will depend on what you want to achieve. You will succeed faster if you include people who:

- have achieved what you want and are willing to share what they know
- share similar business goals or enthusiasm for topics you care about
- believe in you and help you respond constructively at life's ups and downs

To succeed faster you will need to exclude (or minimize) people who drain your energy, make you question your abilities or your goals, or repeatedly make you feel down about yourself. My clients who try to fight this are usually trying to protect relationships that don't feel right for them but that are so long-standing. they don't know how to say goodbye. They're not bad people, but they're keeping my clients down because they're not into personal growth or their aspirations don't match.

If you absolutely must keep somebody in your life, find the things about them that match who you want to be and focus your interactions with them on those things. Ask yourself, "What do I enjoy about this person?" If you enjoy their knowledge of art, talk with them about art exhibits they've recently seen. If you enjoy their knowledge of current events, ask them about what's going on in the world. If you enjoy their knowledge of movies, find out what they've seen and ask what they recommend.

With people who tend to drag your emotions down, the key is to figure out their interests and center your conversations on those interests. Do not talk about your purpose, vision, new values, or meaningful goals with people who you know from past experience are unlikely to be either keenly interested or enthusiastic with their support.

How Tom Fell Behind

A recent client in one of my online group programs—I'll call him Tom—has resisted changing his social, and as a result, his progress has lagged behind other members in his group. Despite admitting that friends and family he sees regularly get him down, despite knowing that he should focus topics of conversation on them, the first thing he did when he made an exciting breakthrough as a result of being in my program was to go and tell those same people. Of course, they did what they do (because they have hot goals, too) and made their predictable deflating and somewhat condescending remarks such as, "Oh, that's nice. We hope that works for you, Tom, unlike all your other things that have fallen through."

I think most of us can relate to and learn from Tom's experience. If you absolutely must keep certain people in your life because you can't imagine cutting them out, then you must change the nature of your conversations. It's critical you don't share your goals and aspirations with people who will not honor them. Find topics that you admire their opinions on, and stay focused on those. Shorten your visits. See them less often. And, critically, fill in the blanks with people who represent where you are headed.

Don't be disappointed with people in your life regardless of how they respond to you. They have the right to be who they are. Expecting them to be one way or another that suits you is as unfair as them expecting you to be one way or another that suits them. What does it mean when people in your life behave in ways that do not align with what you want? Nothing. It means nothing. It means you are not aligned. Neither you nor they are right or wrong. You are expressing your divine right to be yourself, as are they.

Celebrate Individuality!

Celebrate everyone's right to be who they are. Have you ever seen the movie *The Stepford Wives*? It's about a small town in Connecticut populated with eerily similar, robot-like women. It's a chilling satire that illustrates why seeking to be the same is undesirable. I've had several clients who are concerned about people they are "leaving behind" as they create uplifting social circumstances and lives for themselves. They want their loved ones to make the same changes they are making and can get a little pushy as they try to get any resistant family members or friends on board.

In my experience, the best way to have a positive influence on the people you care about is to think of yourself like a magnet. Magnets have two sides, one that attracts and one that repels. If you harangue people in your life about the things they need to change to match who you want them to be, your behavior is like the side of the magnet that repels. If, instead, you let the people in your life be who they are and focus on getting yourself to where you want to be, you are becoming the side of the magnet that attracts.

Freshen Up Your Social

While you are waiting for the people in your life to be irresistibly drawn to your success, you will need to add new social influences into your life that match where you are headed, influences that will help your CTO acclimate to who you want to be. When it comes to your friends and family, you need to focus on the people who make you feel great about who you are and your capacity to achieve anything you set your mind to.

Professionally, you need to find people who have achieved what you want and who will teach you what they know. People who have achieved something that you are looking to achieve are the best ones to ask for advice on how to do it. Everyone else is guessing. In an ideal world, you would be able to find a mentor from whom you can get guidance. Another good option is to join a group or community of people whose goals match yours.

Finding Your Sherpa

Sherpa is the name of a people who live in eastern Nepal and the Himalayas who are known for their mountaineering acumen. If you plan to travel in the area, you would be wise to hire a Sherpa to show you the way. When you're building a business that doesn't fit the model that most people know, you would be well served with a business Sherpa, but how do you find one?

Like my mother prior to jumping off the Dam House roof, I didn't fit in with any group, but in my case, there was no obvious jump to make, mentor to talk to, or group to join. The companies I knew how to build—restaurants, importing, retail, and manufacturing—were based on traditional business models. My peers were consultants and coaches like me, going through the stressful cycle of being either too busy or too slow. My friends with MBAs offered to help, but their knowledge applied to multinational companies. Even the books I read and courses I took taught theories illustrated by completely unrelatable examples drawn from companies, such as Apple, Amazon, eBay, and Uber.

Back then, I had a dream of selling my programs to thousands of people at a time. Since my heroes with business models like this did not sell their services personally to independents like me, I signed up for their online courses. After spending a thousand dollars here and two thousand dollars there and then progressing to spending ten thousand here and fifteen thousand there, I realized that online courses with no, or very little, personalized attention were not working for me.

If you're not familiar with taking online courses alongside hundreds or thousands of others, your only access to expert feedback is on calls where you are lucky to get five to ten minutes of attention during the entire program. You can also comment in Facebook groups, but it's not the expert or highly-trained coach who will respond to you, but often your peers in the group who are encouraged to help you, even as they struggle with the same issues as you.

Faster or Slower

It's no wonder it took me such a long time to build a business I loved. When I first started taking these courses, I was unaware of the pivotal role that hot goals played in my success. Over time, I came to understand that what limited me was not necessarily my goals, nor was it my limiting hot goals. It was a combination of the two.

Business-growth courses that taught me how-to advice alone were not enough for me. When I was stuck on writing my book, I had read several books about how to write books. Knowledge of how to do it was not my problem. My problem was my CTO, Samantha, did not want me to be authentic because if I was authentic, I could get hurt, and she couldn't allow that on her watch.

If you go at it alone, expect a longer learning curve. This has nothing to do with your level of skills or abilities; it has to do with the fact that there's a good chance the lessons you needed most from this book you did not see because your CTO was not ready to let you see them.

We don't become professional photographers the first time we pick up a camera. We don't become a long-distance swimmer the first time we get in a pool. The longer we've been kicking around, the more entrenched our current habits are. If you decide you want to build your business faster, I welcome you to visit www.boom-u.com to see some of our success stories and learn more about how we can help speed up your success.

Ignite: Activate Your Big Idea is for you if you've been wanting to start working for yourself but feel stuck because you need help clarifying your idea and creating your plan of action. With Ignite, we've developed a decision framework that helps you clarify which business idea is best for you, coupled with a business-building framework that helps you step into entrepreneurship informed and empowered.

Basecamp: Increase Your Impact with a Signature Program is for you if you have been selling your services by the hour, your clients love working with you, but your business feels hard to run. With Basecamp, we've developed a system that helps you turn what you know into a teaching or coaching business that makes a predictable income. In both Ignite and Basecamp, we help you identify and reprogram hidden success blocks and show you how to build a profitable business on a shorter timeline.

Follow the system in this book diligently, and you will transition from a job you own to a business you love. If you do this alone, expect to encounter some projects (like my book was for me) that feel out of reach. The process may take you longer, but if you hang in there, then when those setbacks happen, you can remind yourself that where are you are stuck, there is a hot goal that you haven't been able to figure out.

If you do ever get really stuck or, like my mother when she was ten, you just can't bear to let another year go by without getting where you want to be, then I encourage you to visit www.boom-u.com and discover how our programs can help you build the business and life you really want, even faster.

Ready to Climb

You have now learned the final—and unofficial—elements of the all-in system to become unstoppable in business and life: the four most common stumbling blocks my clients have experienced as they implemented the all-in system and how you can learn from their experience to ensure your success.

You were reminded of the importance of committing to a single niche market as you develop your signature program or experience. You've become aware of insidious hot goals that will make some projects harder than others, and if that happens, all is not lost. Instead, you need to dig deeper to find and fix what is blocking you.

You've been alerted to the natural tendency to want to take shortcuts when it comes to the performance equation and why that is such a false economy when in only few minutes you can put it to use to dramatically improve your outcomes. Finally, we explored the power of social, the challenges of honoring relationships from your past that are no longer working for you, and the importance of adding influences that will help your CTO acclimate to who you want to be.

As I said at the beginning of the book, the number one thing you need to succeed with the system is a willingness to return to it and continue using it. Everything that you have achieved in your life and business is the result of actions you have taken. The actions you take each and every day, including what you see, say, and do are the result of hot goals you have set throughout your life.

The older you are, the more established your hot goals are and the more of what you have you will get. This works against you when you don't have what you want. You're becoming unstoppable in the wrong direction.

You can achieve unstoppable success in business and life by applying the all-in system. Each time you reprogram a hot goal for what you want, you take repeated actions in that new direction; eventually taking those repeated actions becomes habit, and you will find yourself living on purpose, expressing your values, and tracking steadily toward your vision.

CHAPTER 13:

It's Go Time

Y ou did it! You went through this journey. You did it because you want more: a business that gives you more than just a paycheck and monopolizes your time and a life that gives you more than the status quo. You wanted more than you were already getting. But no matter the tips, tricks, and hacks, the well-meaning advice from friends and colleagues, the online resources, it just wasn't coming together. It was apparent you had the talent, ability, and work ethic. Still, something was holding you back, something inside that you couldn't reach.

Now that you're here, you can never put the genie back in the bottle. There's no way to pretend the bad habits, repetitive patterns, and blocks you suffered in the past are just who you are. The tools you've learned are at your fingertips. You can program your CTO and get past the obstacles that previously held you back.

You've learned goals are not maybe-someday dreams but laser-focused endpoints with a step-by-step process for reaching them. Who would have

211

thought that identifying future values was vital to building a business that sustains you financially? Did you know coming into this experience that to create a better business, you would have to determine your purpose in the world? Did it seem like a pipe dream that you could increase your productivity without adding more work hours onto your day but by working more strategically?

Some of these ideas may not have been a surprise for you, but I suspect you have never been exposed to an all-in system like this one. I say that because despite my years of tirelessly searching, I had never been able to find one for myself. This is how I came to study, research, practice, and create this system for myself. I wanted to love my work and have a better life—one with purpose, success, and meaning. Once I created the system, I wanted to share it with people like me at age forty-eight. People stuck at basecamp, like I was, but with dreams of scaling the summit.

Rinse and Repeat

The power in this system is that it is rinse and repeat. Seemingly-impossible goals—such as building a business that fits your life—are made possible by a succession of wisely-chosen projects that are well executed. That's what you learned how to do in this book. Explore before you exploit. Right now, you are locked and loaded on a leap project and active assignment. What happens when you complete that assignment? Each time you complete an active assignment (or leap project), return to this system to make your next wise choice and plan of action.

Before You Pick Any New Project

Phase I: Establish Your Current Location

Check in with the ever-changing coordinates of your current location. Take a moment to acknowledge what's working and not working in your life. Remember to acknowledge your CTO for whatever is going well, and be neutral about anything that is still not working. Then, reconnect with your Happiness Recipe, your purpose, vision, and values. Keeping your

Happiness Recipe top-of-mind when making new decisions will keep you moving in a straight line.

Phase II: Clarify Your Target Destination

As you're contemplating your best option for what to do next, consult the Expertise Business Growth Model in Chapter 6 to consider what project would have the greatest leverage for you. Once you have decided what to go after, use the MOMA Method to develop a goal statement that captures the essence of why this goal is important to you, how you will measure success, and start the translation process and programming of a new hot goal.

Phase III: Plans for an Easier Approach

Even when your CTO shares your goal, it is not omniscient. Prime your CTO to know what actions to take by creating a staircase strategy for any leap projects, a nitty-gritty plan for active assignments, and contingency plans for any obstacles you can predict. Critically, this is a great time to reassess any non-productive habitual vices, reevaluate your environmental and social influences, and make a thorough plan for how you will empower yourself by addressing them.

Phase IV: Practices to Speed Up Ascension

Reflect on how much effort or willpower you have been drawing upon to work on what matters most to you. If you are not yet automatically working toward what matters most, recommit to your dopamine-producing practices of doing Thinking Vitamins every morning, writing Happygrams and making your to-do lists each evening, and doing reviews once a week. This would be a good time to refresh your recovery protocols and list of favorite pick-me-ups, too.

Your Success Is Mathematical Law

It's not wishful thinking that you will be unstoppable if you commit to using this system until your CTO takes over. Like any new routines to which you apply yourself, following this system will go from feeling awkward to feeling automatic.

It's explained by neuroscience. You see, say, and do things that lead to more and more of whatever you have now. Even tiny changes in direction become large. That is how to be unstoppable, to make a small change in a direction that will make a big difference to your life in two to three years. What is working well in your life gets better and better; what isn't working becomes worse as time progresses. When you turn forty, you start to notice this phenomenon more. When you turn fifty, you can't ignore it anymore.

I've seen people use the system in this book to achieve pretty remarkable things. The ones who are the happiest are the ones who enjoyed the process because what ends up feeling good is not the winning itself. Winning is not where the pride comes from; it comes from pushing through and accomplishing something many other people wouldn't have the persistence to do. As they say, "If it was easy, everyone would be doing it."

A lot of books that teach you how to fix your business want to teach you how to have more. In this book, my aim was to show you how to have more than more. More than more is a business that you love. It's a life on your terms. It's a life with purpose that is also a good living.

Why All-In?

When I was struggling to write this book, I returned to the performance equation and created a nickname for the book, which also became my working title. My nickname was "All-In."

After a year and a half of failure, the idea of abandoning this project crossed my mind many times, but I couldn't let myself quit, even though it was embarrassing to keep telling my network I was working on a book that never materialized, even though carving out time to work on it was taking time away from income-generating work. I couldn't let myself give up. It was my go time.

To me, the project stood for taking a stand, for building a business and life I loved, no matter how old I was, and for following through on my commitment to share what I have learned.

- It stood for being authentic and showing up as myself.
- It stood for doing what it took to reprogram my CTO.
- It stood for the need to build businesses around our lives and not the other way around.
- It stood for all the pieces of the puzzle, even if that meant smooshing two books' content into one.
- It stood for seeing the project though, no matter how many times I'd failed to meet my goals.
- It stood for programming my brain for what I wanted, so I'd have no choice but to become unstoppable.

I gave myself no other option but to succeed. That's the idea behind the all-in. The "system" is the process—the series of steps to help you figure out what you want and keep you on track to getting there faster. I wrote this book for everyone who has found themselves in a place they don't want to be. *It's Go Time* is as much about leaving what's not working for you as it is about welcoming what will.

What Does It Mean to Live the Dream?

Do you know what happens when you successfully climb a mountain? Do you expect to pull out a lounge chair, grab a cup of tea, glass of wine, or a beer, and bask in the glory of your accomplishments? Not one client I've ever worked with has ever done that when they reached their ambitious goals. If you're like the people I work with, then you can expect to stop for a moment, smile, pat yourself on the back, and have a look around. And do you know what you will see? Another mountain to climb, the one that was hidden from view by the one you just conquered.

I invite you to embrace your journey the way I did mine. Be all-in, not for where you want to arrive someday, but for the journey that you wouldn't trade for anything. For the stories you really want to tell. For the people you want to share your successes with. For the love of life.

Ready?

Set?

It's *your* go time!

APPENDIX: GOAL-OLOGY

As much as I'd like this naming system I've used in Goal-ology to be consistent with the world, this field is something of a mess, which I think contributes to the widespread confusion about how to achieve challenging goals. Full disclosure: The definitions I offer you in Goal-ology are designed to work with the performance equation in this book.

Let's start by getting the standard definitions out of the way. I have drawn the following definitions from Merriam-Webster online:

Commonly-Used Definitions

Goal: the end toward which effort is directed

I like the term "goal," but the challenge is that few people use it accurately. If you ask people their goals, they will rarely tell you the end toward which an effort is directed; instead, they almost invariably answer the question with something they believe they need to do to achieve their desired outcome, which is not an end goal. I will often use the term "outcome" or "target" in place of the word "goal" to help make it clearer.

Subgoal: a goal that is involved in or secondary to achieving a larger goal

The definition for "subgoal" is clear, which is great. What makes it confusing is that there can be so many of them. For instance, for me, putting a new program online would be a subgoal of my mission to teach success-related education. Furthermore, even putting a program online would include several sub-subgoals and then several sub-sub-subgoals. For instance, sub-subgoals could include choosing the topic, production, and marketing, which in turn would have sub-sub-subgoals of brainstorming possible topics, doing market research, lesson planning, slide development, filming, set planning, post-production, tech set-up, and marketing. The list goes on, and so does the number of subs required to organize all these ideas.

Mission: a specific task with which a person or a group is charged

I love the term "mission." It's so clear that it's something you need to do that's of great importance. The problem with using the term for business owners is it also carries the business meaning of "what you're doing/selling and for whom." Trying to use the term mission to define important projects gets confusing. To keep things simple, I suggest you not use this word unless we are talking about your company mission. (I do not address missions in this book because they are best done after the scope of work you are covering here.)

Project: a planned undertaking

Finally, you have the innocent word "project." What I like about it is how clear it is. What I am less fond of is that it's boring. Somehow, thinking of a planned undertaking just doesn't light my fire. It sounds almost tiring. Critically, I can't imagine getting my CTO to accept a hot goal for such a banal word. Besides, some projects keep your day-to-day running, which can be on the boring side, and then some projects change everything. It's not fair to call them all the same thing. We need your CTO to get excited because the next mission/goal/subgoal/project you are going to choose is your entrance fee to the business and life you've been dreaming about for years.

A New Vernacular

My clients were so frustrated by the terms above and their inconsistent uses that I eventually created a language that would be used for the purpose of implementing my system. Throughout the book, we used the following terms and definitions.

Goal

The endgame or desired outcome of any undertaking, including but not limited to visions, missions, projects, subprojects, subgoals, and sub-subgoals.

- Hot Goals: the goals that your CTO is basing its decisions about what you will notice, say, and do that resulted from prior or past programming.
- MOMA Goal Statement: a statement you develop to describe the endgame of any undertaking that requires multiple steps to complete, including vision, goals, project, subproject, subgoal, and sub-subgoal. MOMA stands for Motivating Outcomes with Measurements that are Aligned with your Happiness Recipe. It helps you get clear on what matters to you, set more exciting goals, and translate your goals to a language your CTO understands.

Project

A planned undertaking that involves multiple subprojects, subgoals, steps, or tasks. There are three categories of projects:

- Leap Projects: planned undertakings aimed at helping you transition your business from basecamp to the summit of talent-based entrepreneurial success
- Subprojects: multi-task initiatives involved in or secondary to achieving a project or leap project
- Sub-subprojects: multi-task initiatives involved in or secondary to achieving a subproject

Proven Business Model

You have a business you enjoy operating that fulfills a need or desire that people, who you can predictably reach without relying solely on referrals, are willing to pay for. Ideally, it is a business that does not require you to work in it, so if need (or desire) be, you could give the business to a family member or sell it.

Purpose

A way of contributing that gives your life meaning and makes you feel intrinsically happy.

- Life Purpose: your individual blueprint for happiness (and an intrinsically hot goal)
- Purpose Acorn: a purpose contender you nurture to see if it will grow into a purpose sapling or oak tree

Subgoal

A goal involved in or secondary to achieving a goal or project

- Sub-Subgoal: multi-task initiative involved in or secondary to achieving a subgoal
- Sub-Sub-Subgoal: multi-task initiative involved in or secondary to achieving a sub-subgoal

Task

A planned undertaking that can be completed with a singular action (such as downloading the free templates for this book from https://www.jillmcabe.com/itsgotime_rabbit.

Vision

- Business Vision: a long-term audacious endgame for your company that is underscored by your purpose and that you can't imagine ever not wanting to achieve. A properly-developed vision will help you outperform the market by up to twelve times; however, only business owners with a proven business model are ready to develop these. This is the level of vision that you want to develop once you are done your exploration phase and are preparing to grow or scale.

- Pathfinder Vision: a description of your ideal working day three years from now. A pathfinder vision is the vision level to create when you are in the startup phase of your business, and you still need to prove your business model

ABOUT THE AUTHOR

J ill McAbe is a bestselling author, high-performance expert, and the Founder and CEO
of BOOM-U, an online business school for
solo-entrepreneurs who want to grow themselves, their income, and their impact.

Jill holds a Master of Arts in Leadership
from Royal Roads University, is a faculty
member at York University's Schulich Executive Education Centre, and a Top Teacher on
the global career-skills platform, Skillshare.

She has been featured by Forbes, Authori-
ty Magazine, Thrive Global, and Bold TV. She is an engaging speaker and
has shared her insights on many popular podcasts, including The Harmon
Brothers, David Meltzer, The Luscious Hustle, and others.

A free ebook edition
is available with the
purchase of this book.

To claim your free ebook edition:

1. Visit MorganJamesBOGO.com
2. Sign your name CLEARLY in the space
3. Complete the form and submit a photo of the entire copyright page
4. You or your friend can download the ebook to your preferred device

Morgan James BOGO™

A **FREE** ebook edition is available for you or a friend with the purchase of this print book.

CLEARLY SIGN YOUR NAME ABOVE

Instructions to claim your free ebook edition:
1. Visit MorganJamesBOGO.com
2. Sign your name CLEARLY in the space above
3. Complete the form and submit a photo of this entire page
4. You or your friend can download the ebook to your preferred device

Print & Digital Together Forever.

Snap a photo

Free ebook

Read anywhere

CPSIA information can be obtained
at www.ICGtesting.com
Printed in the USA
BVHW030504080621
608974BV00001B/5